THEOLOGICAL METHOD IN LUTHER AND TILLICH

Law-Gospel and Correlation

Wayne G. Johnson

UNIVERSITY
PRESS OF
AMERICA

Library of Congress Catalog Card Number: **80-5691**

To Shirley

and to Susan, Scott, Jeffrey, and Jonathan

With grateful appreciation to all from whom I have learned, and especially to Dr. George W. Forell and Dr. James C. Spalding for their encouragement, stimulation, and assistance.

ACKNOWLEDGMENTS

Excerpts from the following, by permission of the
University of Chicago Press: Biblical Religion and
the Search for Ultimate Reality, by Paul Tillich,
copyright 1955; The Protestant Era, by Paul Tillich,
copyright 1957; Systematic Theology, Volumes I, II,
and III, by Paul Tillich, copyright 1951 to 1963.
Excerpts from the following, by permission of The
Westminster Press: Luther: Lectures on Romans, newly
translated and edited by Wilhelm Pauck, Volume XV;
The Library of Christian Classics, copyright 1961;
Luther: Early Theological Works, edited by James
Atkinson, Volume XVI: The Library of Christian Classics,
copyright S.C.M. Press, Ltd., London, 1962; The Gospel
and the Churches, by Wilhelm Niesel, tr. Davis Lewis,
copyright 1962; Authority in Protestant Theology, by
Robert Clyde Johnson, copyright 1959; Living Options
in Protestant Theology: A Survey of Methods, by John
B. Cobb, Jr., copyright 1962; The Divine Imperative,
by Emil Brunner, copyright 1947. Excerpts from The
Secular City, by Harvey Cox, copyright 1965, used by
permission of The Macmillan Company. Excerpts from
the following, by permission of Harper & Row,
Publishers, Inc.: The Dynamics of Faith, by Paul
Tillich, copyright 1957; Ultimate Concern: Tillich
in Dialogue, by D. Mackenzie Brown, copyright 1965;
The Christian Intellectual, by Jaroslav Pelikan,
copyright 1965. Excerpts from the following, by
permission of Charles Scribner's Sons: Our Knowledge
of God, by John Baillie, copyright 1959; The Nature
and Destiny of Man, Volume II, by Reinhold Niebuhr,
copyright 1955; The Eternal Now, by Paul Tillich,
copyright 1963; The Interpretation of History, by
Paul Tillich, copyright 1936 (renewed); The Shaking
of the Foundations, by Paul Tillich, copyright 1948
(renewed). Excerpts from the following, by permission
of Concordia Publishing House: Luther's Works
(American Edition), copyright 1958 ff. Excerpts from
"The Problem of Theological Method," by Paul Tillich,
Journal of Religion, Vol. XXVII, No. 1, January, 1947,
by permission of Journal of Religion. Excerpts from
the following, by permission of Fortress Press: Luther's
Works (American Edition), copyright 1958 ff.;

TABLE OF CONTENTS

CHAPTER I

THE LAW-GOSPEL DISTINCTION IN LUTHER'S THEOLOGY

"Unter und uber dem Nein das tiefe, heimliche Ja."
W.A. XVII/ii, 203.

> He was without doubt the angel of which the
> Apocalypse speaks in Chapter XIV: "And I saw
> an angel flying through the midst of heaven,
> who had an eternal gospel to preach," . . .
> the angel who says: "Fear God, and give glory
> to Him!" These are the two articles of the
> teaching of Martin Luther, the law and the
> gospel, by which the whole Scripture is opened
> and Christ made known as our righteousness and
> eternal life.[1]

In such a manner Bugenhagen, a long time friend and
colleague of Martin Luther, characterized the
reformer on the occasion of Luther's death and
burial in February, 1546. While it is somewhat
beyond the scope of this work to pass judgment upon
Luther's relationship to the angelic realm, yet it
seems that we can follow Bugenhagen in stressing the
centrality of the Law-Gospel distinction, as we
shall designate it, in Luther's theological stance.
The reformer's friend does not stand alone in this
judgment, for it is echoed by many who are on the
leading edge of current Luther research. T. M.
McDonough, O.P., maintains that "the Law-Gospel
doctrine constitutes the very heart and core of his
basic convictions; and that the various parts of
his theology . . . are intimately bound up with
this doctrine."[2] And if we move from an English
work to one published in Germany, we find R. C.
Schultz declaring,

> The distinction between law and gospel was the
> basic principle of reformation theology. Out
> of this basic principle the entire doctrines
> of justification through grace alone, of
> penitance, of simul justus et peccator were

1

constructed. The doctrine of the bondage of the will is to be understood only in correlation with this principle, while the reformation hermeneutic also has its roots in this distinction.[3]

The judgment of such scholars corresponds to Luther's own convictions. In his lectures on St. Paul's Epistle to the Galatians (1531), Luther asserts: "The knowledge of this topic, the distinction between the Law and the Gospel, is necessary to the highest degree; for it contains a summary of all Christian doctrine."[4] While a few paragraphs earlier he exclaims: "Therefore whoever knows well how to distinguish the Gospel from the Law should give thanks to God and know that he is a real theologian."[5] In the light of this emphasis, a clarification of the meaning of the Law-Gospel distinction would be a logical beginning for our work.

Let us allow Luther to pose the distinction for us by drawing from a sermon given in 1525:

> The Law commands and requires us to do certain things. The Law is thus directed solely to our behavior and consists in making requirements. For God speaks through the Law, saying "Do this, avoid that, this is what I expect of you." The Gospel, however, does not preach what we are to do or to avoid. It sets up no requirements but reverses the approach of the Law, does the very opposite, and says, "This is what God has done for you; he has let his Son be made flesh for you, has let him be put to death for your sake."[6]

With this paragraph as a backdrop, let us turn to an elucidation of the two key terms, "Law" and "Gospel," and of their systematic interrelation.

What did Luther mean by "Law"? Briefly, he seems to mean the commands and the demands of God--those things man should do and should not do. To expand on this, Luther means by "Law" those

demands and commands of God which are most clearly
set out in the Ten Commandments of Moses[7] but which
are also written "in the hearts" of all men and
which are expressed in the various structures of
human society. Any extensive reading of Luther's
works will indicate that Luther usually uses the
term "Law" when he is speaking of the commands of
God as they are given in the scriptures, and especially as they are focused in the Ten Commandments.
Indeed, many works on Luther seem to assume this is
the consistent meaning of the term for the reformer.[8]
While this view has some merits for a simplified
overview of Luther's theology, a closer look at his
works indicate that the Decalogue is only one form
of the Law of God. Prior to the revelation of the
Law to Moses, mankind was not totally ignorant of
the Law, since all men had the Law "written" in
their minds and hearts.

> It was not Moses that was the author of the
> Decalogue, but from the foundation of the
> world the Decalogue has been inscribed on the
> minds of all men. . . . For there has never
> been any nation under the sun so brutal or
> barbarous and inhuman as not to be aware that
> God is to be worshipped and loved. . . .
> Similarly with regard to honour and obedience
> toward parents and superiors; likewise they
> detested vices, as is to be seen in the first
> chapter to the Romans. . . . So Moses was
> only as it were the interpreter and illustrator
> of laws written on the minds of all men wher-
> ever they are in the world.[9]

Someone might well ask why the Law had to
be revealed to Moses if it be true that it was already written in the mind of man. Luther would
reply that man's natural knowledge of the Law is
"weak and obscured," and that, furthermore, as men
grew more ungodly it became necessary to set the
Law more firmly in view.[10] But if the Law exists
naturally in the mind of man, and if Moses served
to renew man's recognition of the Law, then a third
stage of clarity is attained when our Lord revealed

the true inwardness of the Law by both his teaching and his example.[11] Jesus' summary of the Law
and the prophets in Matthew 7:12 ("Whatever you
wish that men would do to you, do so to them.") is
also understood to be the summary of the natural
law, which can be stated in still another form: "You
shall love your neighbor as yourself." Luther will
summarize this for us from his 1519 lectures on
Galatians:

> Therefore there is one law which runs through
> all ages, is known to all men, is written in
> the hearts of all people, and leaves no one
> from beginning to end with an excuse, although
> for the Jews ceremonies were added and the
> other nations had their own laws which were
> not binding upon the whole world, but only
> this one, which the Holy Spirit dictates
> unceasingly in the hearts of all. . . .
> Consequently this written law, "You shall love
> your neighbor as yourself," says exactly what
> the natural law says, namely, "Whatever you
> wish that men would do to you (this, of course,
> is to love oneself), do so to them (as is
> clear, this certainly means to love others as
> oneself)." . . . certainly love is the end of
> every law. . . .[12]

Certainly it would be inaccurate to imply
that the content of the Law can be divorced from
its function, yet the focus of Luther's attention
regarding the Law is centered not so much on its
content as on its function. Or perhaps one could
say that the focus is on the function of the Law
because of the content of the Law. A clear description of the functions or uses of the Law for
Luther is to be found in his 1531 lectures on
Galatians at that point where he elaborates on verse
3:19 (Why then the Law?).[13] In answer to this "Why?"
Luther expounds a double use of the Law, the "civil"
use and the "theological" or "proper" use of the
Law. Henceforth, in this work, we shall refer to
them as the "civil" and the "proper" uses.[14]

4

The civil use is that use of the Law in
the area of community life and order. In short,
it is the use of the Law in order to restrain the
wicked. Luther understands the whole world as
under the domination of the devil who drives men
to all kinds of despicable deeds. While somehow
allowing the devil a certain sway in the world,
yet God prevents total chaos by "ordaining magis-
trates, parents, teachers, laws, shackles, and all
civic ordinances" so that the hands of the devil
are somewhat bound and thus he is prevented from
"raging at will."[15] Knowing that there would always
be a great abundance of evil men after the Fall,
God established government and give it power even
over a man's life so that violence and sin might
be held in check. Not only does the government
have the power of taking life for life, but it
should also "punish the disobedience of children,
theft, adultery, and perjury. In short, it should
punish all sins forbidden in the Second Table."[16]

By this civil use of the Law, Luther is
not thinking in terms of fixed codes of laws as
they exist in various political structures, but he
is thinking essentially of the will of God as it
is expressed through such legal structures and
codes. Various relations of authority in which
human beings are placed--parents, children, teachers,
servants, rulers, subjects, etc.--are all to be
understood as various expressions of the Law of
God.[17] Thus Law is woven indelibly into the very
fabric of human existence and the universe itself.
Men may offend against this Law, but they cannot
do it with impunity. The Law, in its civil use,
will not make men good, but it does tend to control
behavior and thus make for some semblance of peace
and harmony in the communities of man. This civil
use of the Law applies to all peoples, not to any
elect group; indeed, Luther has a warm respect for
the great men of any nation and time who reflect
the knowledge of this universal law.

God wants the Law to be taught, and He Himself
reveals it; nay, He even writes it upon the
hearts of all human beings, as Paul demonstrates

5

in (Romans) 2:15. From this natural knowledge
have originated all the books of the more
sensible philosophers, such as Aesop, Aristotle, Plato, Xenophon, Cicero, and Cato. . . .
It is a good idea to set these books before
uneducated and unruly individuals, that their
wicked impulses may in some measure be counter-
acted through this training.[18]

Let us allow Luther to express himself, now,
as we move on to a consideration of the "proper"
use of the Law:

Therefore the true function and the chief and
proper use of the Law is to reveal to man his
sin, blindness, misery, wickedness, ignorance,
hate and contempt of God, death, hell, judgment,
and the well-deserved wrath of God.[19]

Law, then, in its proper use, not only drives home
to man a knowledge of sin and its dire consequences,
but it actually multiplies sin itself, since it
prompts anger and rebellion in man.[20] To be sure,
it is still the Divine Law to man and as such it
tells man what he must do; but when a man sees the
demand clearly and looks honestly at his own heart
and life, he realizes that he has not fulfilled and
that he cannot fulfill this command which is laid
upon him. The Law, therefore, not only shows us
that we are guilty, but it humbles us; indeed it
crushes us and leads us to despair over our dilemma.
The sense of despair is rooted in a lively sense
of the judging power of God and the awful consequences of the Divine wrath.

/The/ presumption of righteousness is a huge
and a horrible monster. To break and crush
it, God needs a large and powerful hammer,
that is, the Law, which is the hammer of death,
the thunder of Hell and the lightning of
divine wrath. . . . And so when the Law accuses
and terrifies the conscience--"You must do
this or that! You have not done so! Then
you are condemned to the wrath of God and to

6

eternal death!"--then the Law is being
employed in its proper use and for its
proper purpose. Then the heart is crushed
to the point of despair.[21]

Just what the ultimate purpose of this proper use
of the Law may be will be considered when we elaborate more fully the Law-Gospel distinction as such.

While all scholars would acknowledge
Luther's recognition of the civil and proper (first
and second) uses of the Law, there is considerable
disagreement about the place of the "didactic" or
third use of the Law in Luther's scheme. By the
"didactic" or "normative" use of the Law we mean
Law as a guide for the Christian's life. Law, in
this perspective, becomes a norm or a pattern for
Christian living. At this point let us acknowledge
that Emil Brunner understands Luther as asserting
this third use of the Law, although Brunner writes
that "we must teach the usus tertius legis, the
usus didacticus, the instructive function of the
Law, more plainly than Luther did."[22] Brunner
quotes Reinhold Seeberg as saying that "in Luther's
teaching the threefold use of the Law is assumed,"
but Brunner submits that Luther makes "little use"
of the usus tertius and one-sidedly emphasizes the
usus secondus.[23] Wilhelm Niesel follows Brunner's
point of view by stating that while Luther teaches
the first two uses of the Law in the Smalcaldic
Articles, "he did not mean to exclude the normative
meaning of the Law for believers."[24] On the other
hand, such scholars as Watson and Pinomaa seem to
find no third use of the Law at all in Luther's
theology,[25] while Forell omits any reference to
the third use of the Law in his work on the Protestant faith.[26] Later in this chapter we will
want to deal at some length with some of the logical, semantic, and theological problems that
develop if one admits this third use of the Law
into Luther's theological structure. But first,
let us turn to the meaning of "Gospel."

In the mature Luther, the meaning of

7

"Gospel" can be defined in five words: "Christus Gottessohn ist unser Heiland."[27] While the declaration is short, it sums up the core of the New Testament message for Luther--indeed, the entire thrust of the Christian faith. ". . . the Gospel . . . does not teach me what to do . . . but what someone else has done for me, namely, that Jesus Christ, the Son of God, has suffered and died to deliver me from sin and death."[28] The Gospel is that good news which proclaims to us that God, in and through Christ, has forgiven us and has accepted us and has shown Himself gracious to us. "The Gospel is that Word whereby God discloses His inmost heart, manifesting Himself a gracious God, who wills to deal with us, not as an angry Judge, but as a merciful Father."[29] Such is the proper meaning of the Gospel, according to Luther's mature theology.[30]

Having summarized the meanings of "Law" and "Gospel," we now move on to show their relationship; for while Luther insists on making a distinction between Law and Gospel, he never sunders the two entirely but holds them in a creative interrelationship. Law, in its "proper" use (usus secondus, or theological use),[31] is related to the Gospel in that it serves to reveal to man his sin and his desperate situation before God and thus drive him toward and open him up to the message of the Gospel. The Law accuses and terrifies the conscience; the Gospel brings the message of forgiveness, acceptance, and hope. The Law breaks man's presumption of righteousness; the Gospel announces the true righteousness of Christ with which God clothes the sinner. The Law crushes; the Gospel restores. The Law wounds; the Gospel heals. The Law points out the disease and makes it tragically obvious; the Gospel prescribes the healing of God's grace in Christ.[32] Luther describes the interrelation of Law and Gospel in this passage:

/The/ Law is like a stimulus that drives the hungry toward Christ, in order that He may

8

fill them with His benefits. Therefore the
proper function of the Law is to make us
guilty, to humble us, to kill us, to lead us
down to hell, and to take everything from us,
but all with the purpose that we may be justified, exalted, made alive, lifted up to heaven,
and endowed with all things. Therefore it
does not merely kill, but it kills for the
sake of life.[33]

The proper use of the Law, then, is therapeutic,
not punitive. The Law prepares for and is the precondition of the Gospel.

Both the Law and the Gospel must, however,
be understood as the work of God and the Word of
God. Man is addressed by God as surely in the Law
as he is in the Gospel. The Law-Gospel distinction
must not be allowed to degenerate into some type
of Marcionite ontological dualism whereby the threat
of the Law, as an independent negative principle,
is overcome by the message of grace from the Savior
God. Luther's distinction is not grounded in an
ontological dualism, but rather a dual function
in the saving work of God Himself.[34] God's wrath
as it is directed upon sin and the sinner is made
known through the Law, while God's gracious heart
is revealed through the Gospel. Though God's
nature is wholly one of love, he works his work of
wrath as His "strange" work (opus alienum) so that
His "proper," saving work might be accomplished.[35]

In short, we might say that rightly to look
into the terrible mirror of the Law is to
find it, in the end, a dissolving mirror; it
is to find heaven in the very depth of hell,
grace in the very operation of judgement, joy
and peace in believing where there was nothing
but crushing despair. Or, as Luther put it
in a paradox of wonderful vividness: "unter
und uber dem Nein das tiefe, heimliche Ja"
(deeper than the No, and above it, the deep,
mysterious Yes).[36]

9

Elsewhere, Luther states the two aspects of God's work with the clarity of simplicity:

> For God does not want to trouble you in such
> a way that you remain in trouble; . . . But
> He wants to trouble you so that you may be
> humbled and may acknowledge that you need the
> mercy of God and the blessing of Christ.[37]

With his biting prose, there are times when Luther can speak about the Law in highly deprecatory tones and terms. Speaking of Moses as Law-giver, Luther writes: "He /Moses/ is a minister of death, sin, and damnation,"[38] while in his 1545 preface to the Old Testament, Luther comments: "Rightly, then, does St. Paul call the office of Moses a dispensation of sin and death (II Cor. 3:7), for by his law-giving he brings upon us nothing but sin and death."[39] Certainly for the natural man, the man outside of faith and Christ, the Law is looked upon as a burden and a scourge. Reflecting on the experience of the people of Israel before Moses and the mountain of the Law, Luther writes:

> . . . history clearly states that in the very
> hour in which the people heard the Law nothing
> was more hateful to them than the Law, and
> they would have preferred death to hearing the
> Law. When a man's sin has been disclosed by
> the rays that the Law shines into his heart,
> he finds nothing more odious and intolerable
> than the Law. . . . Therefore, their fleeing
> shows the infinite hatred of the human heart
> against the Law and, as a consequence, against
> God Himself.[40]

Yet the Law is not to be seen, finally, in negative terms by the man of faith. Luther, like Paul, can also speak highly and reverently of the Law. "We should endow it with the highest praises and call it holy, righteous, good, spiritual, divine, etc."[41] For Luther, again like Paul, was sensitive to the charge that he abolished the Law and despised the Law.

Thus it is evident that we do not reject the
Law and works, as our opponents falsely accuse
us. . . . We say that the Law is good and useful, but in its proper use, namely, first, as
we have said earlier, to restrain civic trans-
gressions.[42]

Commenting on the question posed in Galatians 3:19
("Why then the Law?"), Luther writes:

If the Law does not justify, . . . it is nevertheless extremely useful and necessary. . . .
It has this value, that grace can have access
to us. . . . The Law . . . does contribute to
justification--not because it justifies, but
because it impels one to the promise of grace
and makes it sweet and desirable.[43]

But while Luther can speak positively about
the Law and the fruitful work of the Law, one can
scarcely scan any of the reformer's works without
noting that he has strong words against the misuse
of the Law. The first and primary error regarding
the use of the Law is the assumption that the Law
provides, in itself, a means of justification--the
assumption that man can make himself acceptable in
the eyes of God by living out the demands of the
Law.[44] Luther often reflects on his own monastic
life as a time when he, too, labored under the
illusion that various acts of piety and good works
would merit for him the grace of God.[45] In retro-
spect, Luther saw such attempts at works—righteousness as leading, on the one hand, to despair, when
one finds it impossible to fulfill the Law, or, on
the other hand, to smugness and hypocrisy among
those who fancy they do fulfill the Law. Therefore, not only does the attempt at works-righteousness fail to unburden the conscience, but also it
compounds one's guilt. The seeking of righteousness by way of works is equivalent to nullifying
the grace of God shown in the Cross of Christ, for
if man can fulfill the Law through his own works,
then "Christ died to no purpose."[46] The road of
works-righteousness cuts squarely across the refor-

11

mation principle of "justification by faith alone,"
and therefore increases the offense against God.

> Therefore to want to be justified by works of
> the Law is to deny the righteousness of faith.
> On this basis, when those who are self-righ-
> teous keep the Law, they deny the righteous-
> ness of faith and sin against the First,
> Second, and Third Commandments, and against
> the entire Law, because God commands that He
> be worshipped by believing and fearing Him. . . .
> they deny the righteousness, the mercy, the
> promises of God; they deny Christ. . . .[47]

The second abuse against the Law is com-
mitted by those Christians who want to dismiss law
entirely from the Christian life.[48] While Luther
was severe in his criticism of those who sought to
justify themselves by way of works, he had a horror
of those who claimed to live above and beyond the
Law.[49] He would prefer to have this antinomian
fringe of the reform movement be subject "to the
tyranny of the Pope than /have/ the holy name of
God be blasphemed on their account."[50]

The Law may not justify; yet it still has
its place in the life of the Christian man. This
place can best be indicated by describing it against
the background of the understanding of the Christian
man as simul justus et peccator (simultaneously
righteous and sinner).[51] Though the Christian man
stands under the umbrella of God's grace and knows
the reality of God's forgiveness in Christ, this
same Christian man can never look upon himself as
without sin. The believer has the assurance of
being right with God even though he is, paradoxically,
still a sinner. The Christian never trusts his own
status of perfection, but only God. Whale eluci-
dates this paradox in piquant phrases:

> We have joy and peace in believing: not
> because we are arrogant or smug or just plain
> stupid; not because we are living in a fool's
> paradise, blind to the sin that is ever before

12

us; but because the Author of our salvation
is trustworthy and unchanging.[52]

Since the Christian lives as a justified
sinner, yet still a sinner, the Law still exists
for him in its proper, theological sense.

We, too, who are now made holy through grace,
nevertheless live in a sinful body. And
because of this remaining sin, we must permit
ourselves to be rebuked, terrified, slain,
and sacrificed by the Law until we are
lowered into the grave. . . . the Law must
in this life constantly be the slaying,
condemning, accusing Law.[53]

Clearly, for the Christian, the Law endures as the
accusing Law throughout life.

The time of Law is when the Law disciplines,
vexes, and saddens me, when it brings me to
a knowledge of sin and increases this. Then
the Law is being employed in its true use,
which a Christian experiences constantly as
long as he lives.[54]

Thus, while the Christian rightly distinguishes
between the Law and the Gospel, he must never sunder
the one from the other lest he fall either into
presumption or despair. While the Christian rejoices
in the Gospel, he remains aware of the judgment of
the Law; and as long as a man knows the judgment
of the Law, the Gospel is still, indeed, good news.

Having earlier alluded to the possible
presence of the "third use" of the Law in Luther's
theology, we now want to investigate this possibility at some length. I wish to defend the following
assertions: (1) Luther's theology, in its expression
and thrust does not incorporate the third use of the
Law; (2) the Law, to be sure, does continue to exist
as Law for the Christian, but its use is always
theological, not normative.[55]

We deny that Luther includes a genuine
third use of the Law, in the first place, on the
basis of his own terminology and explicit statements. In his major theological works Luther never
once mentions this "third" use specifically, while
he explicitly lists the other two uses many times.
On the other hand, it is easy to document at length
the claim that Luther sees the Law as set aside for
the Christian. The following excerpts come from
his extended comments on Galatians 4:27:

> In this way he /Paul/ sets the people of faith
> far above and beyond the Law. . . . the
> Christian who by faith takes hold of the
> benefits of Christ has no Law at all but is
> free of it . . . for those who believe in
> Christ the entire Law, with all its terrors
> and troubles, has been abrogated. . . . This
> does not mean that the conscience does not
> feel the terrors of the Law at all. Of course
> it feels them. But it means that the conscience
> cannot be condemned and brought to the point
> of despair by such things. . . . Therefore the
> entire Law has been abrogated for believers in
> Christ. . . . If you believe in Him, the Law
> is dead for you.[56]

Obviously we need to acknowledge that
Luther's thrust against the Law is here directed
against the Law as a way of righteousness. For
Luther, righteousness via the Law is not a live
option, since no man can fulfill the Law but all
men stand condemned by the Law. However, for the
man of faith the Law no longer condemns, since it
has been abrogated by God's deed in Christ. Yet,
though Luther speaks here of the Law in the theological sense, his bold statements that the Law is
dead for the believer would seem to mean just that.[57]
Therefore, the Law no longer exists as Law for the
Christian, even in the normative sense; although
we must remember that the Law still exists in the
theological sense even for the Christian, who, we
have seen, remains a sinner in the flesh.

Through reading his New Testament, and

especially St. Paul, Luther does conclude that the
Law is to be fulfilled, but such fulfillment is
always a matter of grace, not of a Christian's own
works. McDonough sums it up nicely:

> . . . the Christian is obliged to do what he,
> by himself, cannot do; whereas he is aware of
> his duties and obligations, stemming from his
> faith, he is, at the same time, warned that
> God alone causes in him true obedience and
> trust and fulfills the Law in his members;
> there is no place here for Melanchthonian
> synergism or Roman Catholic merit. His obe-
> dience and trust are the spontaneous fruit or
> result of unmerited righteousness.[58]

Christ fulfills the Law totally; thus he fulfills
it for the Christian.[59] Christ's righteousness
becomes the Christian's righteousness. The good
works which the Christian does are not works of
merit, but the works of adopted sons which issue
out of the spontaneity of a life transformed by
grace. Luther writes:

> We are not free from the Law . . . in a human
> way, but in a divine and theological way, by
> which we are changed and from enemies of the
> Law are made friends of the Law. . . . it is
> the aim of freedom that now we do what is good,
> not from compulsion but gladly and with no
> ulterior motive.[60]

In reflecting on the attitude which characterizes a
Christian's good works, Luther writes:

> . . . the same Law that was formerly hateful . . .
> now becomes delightful, since love is poured
> into our hearts through the Holy Spirit (Rom.
> 5:5). . . . Christ, who fulfills the Law and
> overcomes sin for us, sends the spirit of love
> into the hearts of those who believe in Him.
> This makes them righteous and lovers of the
> Law, not because of their own works but freely
> because it is freely bestowed by Christ.[61]

It seems clear that in his understanding of the Law and the Gospel, Luther is hereby guarding the principle of justification by faith alone, and is also thereby guarding against any kind of legalism and illusory works-righteousness. In the light of this theological stance, I would submit that Enquist is correct when he says, "Because of his doctrine of the divina lex and his evangelical understanding of the commandments, Luther found no need to teach the third use of the Law."[62]

Yet some questions must be raised. How can the third use of the Law be dismissed when Luther so obviously talks in terms of the Christian's fulfilling of the Law--though, to be sure, through Christ? And how can the third use of the Law be set aside when Luther writes in the following manner?

We must have the law not only because it tells us in a legal way what we are obligated to do, but also that we may see in it how far the Holy Spirit has brought us with his work of sanctification.[63]

Or again, one might ask why, if Luther ignores the third use of the Law, he centers down as he does on the Ten Commandments in both of his catechisms?[64] In answer to these questions, we can reply that, in the first place, the dearth of any material in Luther that hints at the Law's third use renders any attempt to bend a few quotations in that direction as questionable. For instance, a far better interpretation of the comments regarding the Law as a measuring rod for sanctification would be to see the Law, even in this case, as functioning in the theological sense, not the normative. The Law still judges our sin and calls us to grace; it does not become a ladder by which we ascend into the atmosphere of sanctity.[65] So it is with Luther's handling of the Commandments. Surely the commandments are to be taught to the faithful, but this implies nothing regarding their normative use. Rather, Luther interprets the Ten Commandments in terms of the Sermon on the Mount, thus deepening their

16

thrust and stressing their theological, not normative, function.[66] Enquist puts it neatly:

> The center of the theology of the catechisms
> is God's redemption of man in Christ manifested
> in the gift of forgiveness and reflected in
> the divine command to live in terms of faith
> and love. . . . Life, in obedience to God's
> commandments, is to be lived out of God's
> goodness, out of the forgiveness of sins.[67]

        Finally, from a semantic point of view,
it seems inappropriate to include the third use of
the Law in Luther's theology. If we take Luther's
meaning of "Law," we see Law as a command or demand
of God which requires fulfillment and which promises
judgment if transgression occurs. Law commands,
and, if unfulfilled, it condemns. Law, to be Law,
requires both aspects. For Luther, however, the
Gospel announces that grace has intervened and the
Law, therefore, is abrogated for the Christian man
in that it no longer condemns But when Law no
longer holds the threat of condemnation, it is no
longer Law, but something else--or nothing.[68]

        Let us give Luther a final word:

> The understanding of this matter lies in
> recognizing and truly distinguishing the Law
> and the Gospel, that you may know that the
> teaching of the Law commands only what is to
> be done by the ungodly and lost, as I Tim. 1:9
> says: "The Law is not laid down for the just
> but for the lawless." But where the godly
> are, there the Law, which is intended only for
> the humiliation of the ungodly through the
> recognition of their sin and weakness, is
> already abolished. The Gospel teaches from
> what source you receive the power to fulfill
> the Law. In this respect it commands nothing;
> nor does it force the spirit, which hastens
> of its own accord by faith. It adds some
> commands, but it does so to kill the remnants
> of the old man in the flesh, which is not yet

17

justified. From these commands, however, the
spirit is free, being satisfied with faith
alone. Of this matter we have spoken amply
elsewhere.[69]

In summary, it seems that Luther's refusal
to embrace the third use of the Law saves him from
two dangers. First, it saves him from a threatening
legalism which hovers over Calvin's theology.[70]
Secondly, it saves him from the danger of losing
the important distinction between the Law and the
Gospel altogether, as Palmer implies of Barth's
theological efforts.[71] Luther, I feel, negotiates
these dangerous waters rather neatly and effectively.
However, the history of the Lutheran movement has
tended to fulfill Luther's own fears that after his
time the Law-Gospel distinction "will be obscured
again and completely wiped out."[72] But in spite of
the vagaries of history, it remains clear that Luther
clearly and consistently honors his distinction and
thereby guards his entire theological structure.

FOOTNOTES

1. Ernst Wolf, Martin Luther (Theologische Existenz Heute, Heft 6, Munich, 1934), p. 7, quoted by Wilhelm Pauck, The Heritage of the Reformation (Glencoe: Free Press of Glencoe, Inc., 1961), p. 19.

2. Thomas M. McDonough, O.P., The Law and the Gospel in Luther (London: Oxford University Press, 1963), p. 3.

3. R. C. Schultz, Gesetz und Evangelium in der lutherischen Theologie des 19. Jahrhunderts (Berlin: Lutherisches Verlagshaus, 1958), p. 11. My translation of the text.

4. Martin Luther, Luther's Works (St. Louis: Concordia Publishing House/Philadelphia: Muhlenberg Press, 1955--), XXVI, 117, (1531). Hereafter, this work will be cited as A.E. (for American Edition), followed by volume number, page, and the date of composition of the original work in parenthesis.

5. A.E., XXVI, 115, (1531).

6. A.E., XXXV, 162, (1525). From a sermon entitled "How Christians Should Regard Moses."

7. We should note that Luther understands all of the Old Testament laws as being from God through Moses--both the Decalog and the ceremonial. This total law applied to the nation of Israel, and this total law has been set aside, as a means of righteousness, by Christ's work. The ceremonial laws were given only to the Jews. Only those aspects of Old Testament law which are parallel to the "natural law" are binding on the Gentiles. See A.E., XXVI, 121 ff. (1531), and Julius Kostlin, The Theology of Luther (2 vols.; Philadelphia: Lutheran Publication Society, 1897), II, 36 and 232 ff.

8. McDonough, op. cit., in his introductory chapter, generally equates "Law" with "Decalog." In his chapter "The Paradox of Law and Gospel," in The Protestant Tradition (Cambridge: Cambridge University Press, 1955), J. S. Whale speaks of the Law as the Ten Commandments intensified by the focus on inward disposition revealed in the Sermon on the Mount.

9. Martin Luther, D. Martin Luther Werke. Kritische Gesamtausgabe (Vols. I ff.; Weimer, 1883 ff.), XXXIX/1, 454, as cited by Philip Watson, Let God Be God! (Philadelphia: Muhlenberg Press, 1947), p. 98. Hereafter citations from the Weimer edition will be listed as W.A., with volume and page following.

10. W.A., XXXIX/1, 361: "All men indeed have naturally a certain knowledge of the law, but it is very weak and obscured. Hence it was and always is necessary to hand down to men that knowledge of the law that they may know the greatness of their sin. . . . W.A., XXXIX/i, 454: ". . . since men had come at length to such a pitch that they cared neither for God nor for men, God was compelled to renew those laws through Moses, and to set them before our eyes written with His finger on tables. . . ." Cited by Watson, op. cit., p. 99.

11. Watson, op. cit., pp. 105-106, makes this development.

12. A.E., XXVII, 355, (1519); Cf. A.E., XXVII, 56, (1531); A.E. LI, 106, (1522). For a good summary of this "unity" of the Law see Lennart Pinomaa, Faith Victorious (Philadelphia: Fortress Press, 1963), p. 145.

13. A.E., XXVI, 314 ff. (1531).

14. The "civil" or "political" use of the Law is also commonly referred to as the "first" use, while the "proper" use is labelled as the "second" use. Luther may also refer to the "proper" use as the "theological," "spiritual," or the "true" use of the Law.

15. A.E., XXVI, 308-309 (1531).

16. A.E., II, 141, (1535 ff.).

17. Watson, op. cit., p. 155. Watson points out that this does not imply that such structures of ruling power cannot err. The "offices" can be abused; and the laws expressed through these offices are valid only insofar as they are in harmony with the natural and Divine Law.

18. A.E., II, 160, (1535 ff.).

19. A.E., XXVI, 309, (1531).

20. Martin Luther, Luther: Lectures on Romans (1515-1516), Vol. XV of "Library of Christian Classics" (Philadelphia: Westminster Press, 1961), pp. 209-210.

(Hereafter this work will be cited as L.C.C., XV.)
Here Luther expands upon Romans 7:8, "Without the
Law sin was dead." See also A.E., XXVI, 341, (1531).
    21. A.E., XXVI, 310, (1531).
    22. Emil Brunner, The Divine Imperative, trans.
Olive Wyon (Philadelphia: The Westminster Press,
1947), p. 149.
    23. Ibid., p. 605, note 6 on Chapter XIV.
    24. Wilhelm Niesel, The Gospel and the Churches,
trans. David Lewis (Philadelphia: The Westminster
Press, 1962), p. 216. Niesel rightly points out
that the third use of the Law is expressed in the
"Formula of Concord" (1577), but this is hardly a
cogent argument in favor of Luther's use of the Law
in this way.
    25. Watson, op. cit., pp. 155 ff.: Pinomaa, op.
cit., pp. 73 ff.
    26. George Forell, The Protestant Faith (Engle-
wood Cliffs, New Jersey: Prentice-Hall, Inc., 1960),
pp. 94 ff.
    27. "Christ the Son of God is our Savior."
Quoted by Whale, op. cit., p. 23. Whale does not
give the source.
    28. A.E., XXVI, 91 (1531).
    29. Watson, op. cit., p. 157.
    30. The Luther of before the indulgence contro-
versy sometimes spoke in terms of a Gospel that had
two sides--Law and grace. Kostlin, op. cit., I, 110,
shows that in Luther's "First Exposition of the
Psalms: (1513) the Gospel envelopes both a sense of
Law and a sense of grace. Gordon Rupp, in his The
Righteousness of God (London: Hodder and Stoughton,
1953), pp. 154-155, correctly points out that in
these early lectures on the Psalms Luther had not
yet arrived at the type of Law-Gospel dynamic and
relation which becomes normative in such a mature
work as his famous 1531 commentary on Galatians.
It is somewhat surprising, therefore, to find that
Watson, op. cit., pp. 156-159, writes as if this
"two-office" view of the Gospel is Luther's general
position. Watson cites only very early works of
Luther to make his point, and seems to be unaware
of a shift away from this perspective in Luther's
mature works. Already in his commentary on Romans
(1515-1516), L.C.C., XV, 199, Luther indicates that

21

the "full sense" of Gospel is where it "preaches Christ"--i.e., grace and forgiveness of sin. Certainly in his mature works "Gospel" is always and only seen as grace, never as Law. Cf. A.E., XXVI, 91 and 208-209, (1531).

31. Hereafter we shall use "Law" in this "proper" sense, since it is by far the most significant use of the Law for Luther. It is this aspect of the Law which concerns us in this work.

32. A.E., XXVI, 310, (1531): Martin Luther, "Smalcald Articles," The Book of Concord, ed. and trans. Th. Tappert (Philadelphia: Muhlenberg Press, 1959), Part III, Article iii; Whale, op. cit., 22 ff.; Watson, op. cit., pp. 171 ff.; A.E., XXVI, 132-133, 348, (1531).

33. A.E., XXVI, 345, (1531).

34. For a discussion of Luther's "dualism" from the standpoint of the Swedish theologians, see Edgar Carlson, The Reinterpretation of Luther (Philadelphia: Westminster Press, 1948), pp. 48-57. Carlson summarizes (p. 57): Luther's dualism "may be described as an empirical dualism which arises out of the factual data of experience and which is verified in the culminating and decisive revelatory event--namely the cross."

35. Pinomaa, op. cit., pp. 17 ff.; Carlson, op. cit., pp. 48 ff.; Whale, op. cit., pp. 23 ff.; Kostlin, op. cit., II, 289 ff.; A.E., XXVI, 38, (1531); A.E., II, 134, (1535--); A.E., XIV, 335, (1518).

36. Whale, op. cit., pp. 40-41. Whale rightly points out that not all of God's work is salvatory; there is that ira severitatis which punishes and destroys--as the wrath of perdition.

37. A.E., XXVI, 339, (1531).

38. A.E., XIII, 79, (An exposition of Psalm 90 in 1535).

39. A.E., XXXV, 242, (1545).

40. A.E., XXVI, 320, (1531). Here we find Luther describing the psychological dynamics of Nietzsche's Ugliest Man, the one who killed God because God saw man's hidden disgrace and ugliness. F. Nietzsche, Thus Spoke Zarathustra, trans. R. Hollingdale (Baltimore: Penguin Books, 1961), pp. 278-279.

41. Ibid., p. 365.

42. Ibid., pp. 312-313.
43. Ibid., pp. 314-315.
44. Ibid., pp. 344, 400.
45. Ibid., p. 70.
46. Ibid., pp. 181-182.
47. Ibid., pp. 253-254.
48. Ibid., p. 344.
49. B. A. Gerrish, Grace and Reason (Oxford: The Clarendon Press, 1962), p. 102.
50. A. E., XXVI, 306, (1531). Needless to say, Luther was deeply concerned about the disrepute this antinomian fringe could bring upon the whole reform movement.
51. Ibid., 232 ff.
52. Whale, op. cit., p. 81.
53. W. A., LI, 440, (1535). Quoted in E. Plass, What Luther Says (Vols. I-III; St. Louis: Concordia Publishing House, 1959), II, 770.
54. A. E., XXVI, 341, (1531).
55. Our stand is opposed, at least in part, in the following works: Robert C. Johnson, Authority in Protestant Theology (Philadelphia: Westminster Press, 1959), p. 34; Brunner, op. cit., p. 605; Niesel, op. cit., p. 216. On the other hand, Kostlin finds little evidence to support such a third use of the Law in Luther (op. cit., I, 191; II, 501-502); and Werner Elert in his The Christian Ethos, trans. Carl Schindler (Philadelphia: Muhlenberg Press, 1957), pp. 294 ff., concludes that Luther did not employ this third use of the Law though Melanchthon found it appropriate as a guard against libertinism.
56. A. E., XXVI, 445 ff., (1531). Underlining mine.
57. Contrast the general atmosphere of John Calvin's view in his Institutes of the Christian Religion, trans. F. L. Battles (Philadelphia: Westminster Press, 1960), Book II, Chapter vii. For Calvin, the third use of the Law is the principle use; thus the Law still stands for the Christian, although it is abrogated in the sense that it no longer condemns. For a good summary of what Luther means by freedom from the Law see Kostlin, op. cit., II, 497 ff.
58. McDonough, op. cit., p. 94, note 1.

59. A. E., XXVI, 324, (1531).
60. A. E., XXVII, 347, (1519).
61. A. E., XXVII, 326, (1519).
62. Roy Enquist, "The Living God: A Study of
the Contemporary Discussion of Law and Gospel in
Lutheranism" (an unpublished Ph.D. dissertation
from Union Theological Seminary, 1960), p. 31.
Here Enquist is rebutting Barth's and Reinhold
Niebuhr's charge of quietism against Luther's theological ethics.
63. W. A., L, 643, as quoted by Johnson, op.
cit., p. 34. Johnson quotes this segment to buttress
his contention that Luther reflects Calvin's third
use of the Law. Johnson is, I think, moving on
slim evidence incorrectly interpretated.
64. Niesel, op. cit., p. 216. Here Niesel
asserts that Luther, in his Small Catechism, expounds
the Ten Commandments as the "normative meaning of
the Law for believers." I submit that this is seeing
Luther through Barthian spectacles.
65. At this point we can turn Luther's
arguments against Erasmus to our cause. Erasmus
argued that a command logically implied the ability,
on man's part, to fulfill the command. "Not so,"
replied Luther. "How is it that you theologians
are twice as stupid as schoolboys, in that as soon
as you get hold of a single imperative verb you
infer an indicative meaning, as though the moment
a thing is commanded it is done, or can be done?"
(Bondage of the Will, trans. Packer and Johnston
Westwood, N. J.: /Fleming H. Revell Co., 1957/,
p. 159). Luther goes on to assert that the imperative
of the Law is designed to serve the theological
function of the Law. So, also, I would argue that
when Luther recommends the Commandments as a "measure"
for sanctification, he still uses the Law in its
theological, not the normative, sense.
66. Cf. George Forell, Faith Active in Love
(Minneapolis: Augsburg Publishing House, 1954),
p. 159.
67. Enquist, op. cit., p. 23.
68. This "something else" might well be a type
of "image" or "ideal" which beckons the Christian
onward, but which does not demand as such. Thus
through faith the Ten Commandments are changed from

the "accusing Law to a description of the possibilities of the Christian life." So concludes George Forell, _Ethics of Decision_ (Philadelphia, Muhlenberg Press, 1955), p. 104. Schleiermacher notes that "Christian Ethics" should drop the "imperative mood" and simply give "an all-round description of how men live within the Kingdom of God." _The Christian Faith_, ed. by MacKintosh and Stewart (2 vols.; Harper Torchbooks; New York: Harper and Row, 1963), II, 524.

69. A. E., IX, 179-180, (1525).
70. Cf. Brunner, _op. cit._, p. 605, note 6 on chapter XIV.
71. Russell Palmer, "Karl Barth and the Orders of Creation: A Study in Theological Ethics" (an unpublished Ph.D. dissertation from the University of Iowa, 1966), p. 76.
72. A. E., XXVI, 312, (1531). See George Forell's article, "The State As Order of Creation," _God and Caesar_, ed. W. Quanbeck (Minneapolis: Augsburg, 1959), pp. 29-52, for an indication of how the Law-Gospel distinction was lost in the area of civil authority. Jerald Brauer, in "We Have This Ministry," _Lutheran Social Welfare Quarterly_, V (December, 1965), pp. 3-39, asserts: "The hard historical fact remains that Lutheranism did drive a wedge between the Law and the Gospel and tended to abdicate responsibility for the proclamation and application of the Law to the total life of society." Brauer goes on to say that since history failed to sustain the proper distinction in the past, the current attempt among some Lutheran theologians toward redeveloping the proper form of the distinction will probably fail!

CHAPTER II

PAUL TILLICH'S METHOD OF CORRELATION

". . . man cannot receive answers to questions
he has never asked."
Systematic Theology, I, 65.

Tillich's was a complex mind. Serious
critics and supporters alike speak unanimously of
his massive learning and his creative thinking,
even though many would not follow him in walking
the "tight-rope" boundary line between philosophy
and theology.[1] In this work there will be no attempt
at developing the complexity of Tillich's thought,
rather we shall seek to elucidate his method of
correlation and explore some of the assumptions
intimately related to this Method.[2] To be sure,
any attempt to isolate one segment of Tillich's
theology, or even the Method itself, is fraught
with difficulty, since his theology is organismic--
in the sense that there is an inherent interrelation
among the many facets of his thinking. To isolate
a part of Tillich's theology, then, from the whole
of the living "organism" is to run the danger of an
abstraction which has no life in and of itself.
Yet a complete overview of either Tillich or Luther
is impossible in a work of this scope; thus the
attempt at abstraction will be made, hoping there
are sufficient ties made to the organism to grant
clarity and comprehension.

Before we describe the Method, an exploration of several facets of Tillich's thought may be
helpful. At the outset Tillich's understanding of
religion itself needs to be seen as soteriological.
Religion is a matter of salvation; and Christianity,
especially, has been "rightly called a religion
of salvation."[3] The concept of salvation has always
been at the heart of the Christian message, although
an attempt to recapture the genuine meaning of the
word must be made. Throughout Christian history
the genuine meaning of salvation has often been
pushed into the background, while a focus on

27

salvation as "ultimate fulfillment of the individual beyond time and history," or on salvation as "the conquest of special sins and progress toward moral perfection" or on salvation as "the conquest of the godless state through conversion and transformation" has developed.[4]

A more adequate understanding of the original meaning of salvation is to be found in the root word salvus which means healed or whole.[5] "The saviour makes 'heal /sic/ and whole' what is sick and disrupted."[6] While such terms carry a strong connotation of bodily infirmity, Tillich wants to move beyond this suggestive metaphor toward an understanding of a healing which involves a more ultimate negativity. One can be "saved" from any number of "negativities"--forces and situations which threaten our existence, or, better, our being-ness, in one form or another. But the ultimate negativity can be called "condemnation or eternal death, the loss of the inner telos of one's being, the exclusion from eternal life."[7] The question of salvation gets its weight and its power from this understanding of the term; to reduce the term to a matter of morals or to the promise of heaven is to weaken its thrust and undercut its relevance.

Not only is religion to be understood as salvatory, but also as "ultimate concern." Indeed one could say that religion involves ultimate concern because it does deal with salvation in its depth meaning. But what is "ultimate concern"? At one point Tillich would define it as "the abstract translation of the great commandment: ' . . . you shall love the Lord your God with all your heart, and with all your soul, and with all your mind, and with all your strength.'"[8] In the context of a discussion with college students, Tillich states,

I have sometimes explained it successfully, . . . as taking something with ultimate seriousness, unconditional seriousness. . . . What, for instance, would you be ready to suffer or even die for?
. . . .

28

It is not life and death in that sense /being
willing to die for a cause/ that I mean, but
in the sense of Hamlet's 'To be or not to be,'
which does not mean either to die or to live
a few years longer, but to find an answer to
the ultimate question of the meaning of life.[9]

In a more technical discussion he explicates religion
as "the state of being grasped by an ultimate concern,
a concern which qualifies all other concerns as
preliminary and which itself contains the answer
to the question of the meaning of our life."[10] Such
concern is independent of "conditions of character,
desire, or circumstance." It is total concern in
the sense that no part of our own experience--emotional,
intellectual, volitional--or no part of our world
can be excluded from it.[11] The concern of religion,
then, deals with the final concerns of life and its
meaning. All other concerns are preliminary and,
therefore, are not religious concerns--unless they
become idolatrous by being shifted, falsely, to
ultimacy.[12] In short, Tillich asserts that religion,
in its most significant sense, deals with the
"whence, why, and whither" of life, not with "how"
and "what."

Tillich would grant that the term "ultimate
concern" is ambiguous; in fact, he indicates that
it is intentionally so since it may refer either to
an object or to a state. "It indicates, on the one
hand, our being ultimately concerned--the subjective
side--and on the other hand, the object of our ultimate concern, for which of course there is no other
word than 'ultimate.'"[13] The entire history of
religion, in the light of this double meaning, is
the history of man's subjective involvement in an
attempt to find what can be accepted as the object,
the ultimate, which most religions refer to as
"God." This would imply that we must make a logical
distinction between the concept of ultimate concern
and the content of ultimate concern. Indeed, since
ultimate concern is an "abstract translation" of
the great commandment, one can best look upon it
as a formal concept without any specific content in

its own right. This understanding of religion
allows Tillich not only to take a positive stance
toward the phenomenon of religion in human history,
in contrast to Barth, Brunner, and Bonhoeffer, but
also to use this understanding of religion as a
point of contact for a dialogue with persons from
non-Christian traditions.[14]

Tillich's understanding of faith is
intimately related to his conception of religion;
indeed, the concepts at times appear to be synonymous.
A cluster of his definitions may be a good starting
point for developing his understanding of the term.
"Faith is the state of being ultimately concerned."
"Faith is a total and centered act of the personal
self, the act of unconditional, infinite, and
ultimate concern." "Faith is participation in the
subject of one's ultimate concern with one's whole
being."[15] In another work this definition is offered:
"Faith is the state of being grasped by an ultimate
concern. . . . Faith is the concern about our
existence in its ultimate 'whence' and 'whither.'"[16]

Faith understood as being ultimately
concerned is a "centered act" which involves every
aspect of a man's personality. "If one of the
functions which constitute the totality of the
personality is partly or completely identified with
faith, the meaning of faith is distorted."[17] In
keeping with the understanding of faith as a
centered act, Tillich would guard the meaning of
faith from three distortions. The intellectualistic
distortion of faith occurs when faith is misunderstood as an act of knowledge "that has a low degree
of evidence." Faith becomes a matter of accepting
certain information as true, whether it be Biblical
records, or classical creedal statements or the
dogmatic assertions of an authoritative ecclesiastical
body.[18] In this stance, faith tends to be reduced
to mental assent, therby deleting the aspect of
fiducia or living trust and undercutting the
existential character of faith.

A second possible misunderstanding of faith

30

is the voluntaristic distortion, which occurs when faith is seen basically as an act of the will which brings one to the point of accepting certain formulas as true. This voluntaristic distortion leans back upon the intellectualistic, yet is distinguished from it in that the former accents the role of the will while the latter accents the role of the mind. This second distortion, Tillich points out, can be found in both the Roman Catholic and Protestant traditions.[19]

The third distortion of faith, the emotionalistic, is to be found mainly in Protestant thinking. Here faith is understood as merely a matter of subjective emotions without any specific content and without any particular demands. This effectively puts religion into a subjective corner of experience and cuts it off from all claims to truth and thus from a living interaction with culture.[20]

While Tillich names these possible distortions of faith, he does not deny the proper place of the three aspects of personality thereby involved. Indeed, faith seen as the ultimate concern of the whole man implies that will, intellect, and emotions are involved in the faith stance. Anything less does not claim the whole man. Anything less is not faith seen as ultimate concern.

An especially existential note in Tillich's thought comes through when he discusses the relationship between faith, risk, and doubt. A formative role in this aspect of Tillich's thinking was played by his teacher Martin Kahler, whose stress on justification by faith brought a new insight to his pupil.

> The step I myself made in these years /under Kahler/ was the insight that the principle of justification through faith refers not only to the religious-ethical but also to the religious-intellectual life. Not only he who is in sin but also he who is in doubt is justified through faith.[21]

Faith, then, is not to be seen as the antithesis

31

of doubt.

> Faith and doubt do not essentially contradict
> each other. Faith is the continuous tension
> between itself and the doubt within itself.
> This tension does not always reach the strength
> of a struggle; but, latently, it is always
> present. This distinguishes faith from logical
> evidence, scientific probability, tradition-
> alistic self-certainty, and unquestioning
> authoritarianism.[22]

There is an element of uncertainty in faith which
cannot be removed and which must be accepted through
that element in faith Tillich designates as courage.
This element in faith is necessary because in every
act of faith there is a possibility of failure, a
risk which is carried through courage. The risk of
faith is the risk that the concrete content of our
ultimate concern may, in fact, prove to be a matter
of preliminary and transitory concern. Tillich
cites "nation" or "success" as such possible preliminary concerns which cannot stand the strain of
ultimate commitment.

> The risk to faith in one's ultimate concern
> is indeed the greatest risk man can run. For if
> it proves to be a failure, the meaning of one's
> life breaks down; one surrenders oneself,
> including truth and justice, to something which
> is not worth it. One has given away one's
> personal center without having a chance to
> regain it. . . . If faith is understood as being
> ultimately concerned, doubt is a necessary
> element in it. It is a consequence of the risk
> of faith.[23]

At this point we should briefly explore the
metaphor "being grasped," which is involved in
Tillich's understanding of faith as ultimate concern.
By this metaphor Tillich does not necessarily mean
a dramatic personal experience of conversion; rather,
he uses the phrase to indicate that faith as a state
of being ultimately concerned is not produced by us,

but is found <u>within</u> us as something <u>given</u> to us.[24]
This seems to be a transparent restatement of the
Pauline doctrine of faith as a gift, not a work.
In replying to a charge of implicitly denying free
will by the use of such a metaphor, Tillich says:

> But to speak of <u>free</u> will, we ourselves never
> make the decision /i.e., our ultimate concern/
> in this respect; it never comes from ourselves.
> If it did, it would not be ultimate. We would
> be making the decision immediately as some-
> thing we could revoke at any moment. . . . I
> think Luther's description of the experience
> is psychologically much sounder, although he
> did not deny the freedom of participating in
> it with our whole personality--which in fact
> <u>means</u> freedom. On the other hand, he knew
> well from his own experience that we ourselves
> cannot produce the ultimate concern, and this
> is what "being grasped" means.[25]

One of the intriguing implications of
Tillich's definition of faith and religion as
"ultimate concern" is the universality and necessity
of faith and/or religion. These formal definitions
apply to all of the great world religions and even
to the "quasi-religions," such as Fascism and
Communism.[26] Each religion demonstrates an ultimate
concern in the subjective sense, and holds to an
ultimate concern in the objective sense. Of course
this does not imply that all faiths are, therefore,
"true" or adequate or justifying; but it does imply
that the only existing alternatives are a genuinely
"ultimate" concern or idolatry.[27] Furthermore, since

> . . . faith is not a phenomenon besides others,
> but the central phenomenon in man's personal
> life . . . its existence is necessary and
> universal. . . . If faith is understood as
> what it centrally is, ultimate concern, it
> cannot be undercut by modern science or any
> kind of philosophy. . . . Faith stands upon
> itself and justifies itself against those who
> attack it, because they can attack it only in
> the name of another faith. It is the triumph

33

of the dynamics of faith that any denial of
faith is itself an expression of faith, of
an ultimate concern.[28]

With the above material providing a general
orientation for viewing Tillich's theologizing, let
us now look more specifically at his understanding
of the task of theology and of theological method.
The dialectic nature of Tillich's Method is reflected
in the very first paragraph of his Systematic Theology.
He writes: "A theological system is supposed to
satisfy two basic needs: the statement of the truth
of the Christian message and the interpretation of
this truth for every new generation."[29] That is to
say, theology must deal adequately with the eternal
truth of the foundations of the Christian faith, but
it must also seek to understand and speak to the
temporal situation where the message is to be
received. Fundamentalism or orthodoxy errs in
failing to make contact with the present situation.[30]
On the other hand the "so-called German Christians"
and the "religious progressivism of the so-called
humanists in America" err by "losing themselves in
the relativities" of their own particular situation.[31]
Tillich intends to be both adequate and relevant
by charting a course which keeps in contact with
both the kerygma (the unchangeable truth of the
message) and the changing demands of each historical
situation.

This means that there must always be an
apologetic aspect to theology since "kerygmatic
theology needs apologetic theology for its completion."[32]
While recognizing that some forms of apologetics have
been "weak and disgusting," Tillich asserts that only
an apologetic theology can be an "answering theology"--
a theology that listens to the "situation" and
answers the questions implied in the situation.
Without this "listening" and "answering" aspect,
theology loses its apologetic pole and must resort
to "throwing" the message of the kerygma "like a
stone" into the situation.[33]

In his discussion of the nature of systematic theology, Tillich insists that one cannot

34

elaborate a theology as an "empirical-inductive or
a metaphysical-deductive 'science,' or as a combi-
nation of both. . . ."[34] Theology can never become
a "science" because in the end the issue is decided,
at least in part, by individual experience, valuation,
and commitment. "Every understanding of spiritual
things (Geisteswissenschaft) is circular."[35] What
Tillich seems to mean is that every theologian or
every religious philosopher must step into and do
his thinking within a "circle" determined by a
cluster of presuppositions which have been "given"
to him and made real to him through his own
experience. Thus theology is always a matter of
commitment, whether recognized or unrecognized.[36]

          This circular nature of theology is
reflected in the two "formal criteria" of every
theology, and at the same time we find these two
criteria leaning back upon Tillich's understanding
of the nature of religion and faith.[37] These
criteria are called "formal" since they do not deal
with the content of the theology as such, but are
"abstracted from the concrete materials of the
theological system."[38] I take this to mean that
the formal criteria apply to and are descriptive
of the theological endeavor in general, but not
to the specific content or specific details of
theological material. Tillich presents the first
criterion: "The object of theology is what concerns
us ultimately. Only those propositions are theological which deal with their object insofar as it can
become a matter of ultimate concern for us."[39] The
negative implication of this criterion is that
theology should never presume to speak authorita-
tively in the area of preliminary concerns such as
physics, art, and medicine; rather its focus is on
ultimate concern.

          The second criterion he offers is, in
reality, an elaboration of the first: "Our ultimate concern is that which determines our being or
nonbeing. Only those statements are theological
which deal with their object insofar as it can become a matter of being or not being for us."[40] In
this context the term "being" does not designate

our human existence within the world of time and
space, rather it refers to "the whole of human
reality, the structure, the meaning, and the aim
of existence."[41] This is our being which is
threatened, our being which can be saved or lost.
The object of theology, then, is that which determines our ultimate destiny beyond all other concerns
which are preliminary and accidental. Theology
deals with that which finally sustains our existence
in terms of our meaning, our aim, and our end.

While the broadest sense of the word
"theology" means "the _logos_ or the reasoning about
theos (God and divine things)," Tillich puts the
following forward as his primary definition:
"Theology is the methodical interpretation of the
contents of the Christian faith."[42] It seems fair
to observe that the latter definition is not a formal
definition of theology in general, but a specific
definition of _Christian_ theology. The implication
here is that there are theologies that are not
Christian theologies. Certainly this is no
astounding observation and it is fully in keeping
with the universality and necessity of religion
and/or faith, as Tillich sees it, which are
expressions of man's nature as man. Where there is
man, there is religion as ultimate concern; thus
where there is man there is theology, though often
elaborated mythically and speculatively.[43] The
special task of _Christian_ theology, within this
context, is to demonstrate by way of apologetics
that the trends "which are imminent in all religions
and cultures move toward the Christian answer."[44]
Christian theology necessarily claims to be _the_
theology. This claim can be defended from the standpoint of the incarnation. For in the incarnational
event the absolutely concrete (the personal life
manifested in the event "Jesus as the Christ") and
the absolutely universal (the Logos, the principle
of divine self-manifestation) meet and merge at a
point. This is the point "which is described as
the 'Logos who has become flesh.'"[45]

While a detailed consideration of the place
and role of reason in both Luther's and Tillich's
thought will be presented in later chapters, we must

36

give momentary consideration to Tillich's understanding of philosophy in order to describe the
Method with some clarity. If the theologian is
to assert, as Tillich maintains he must, that he
deals with a special realm of knowledge, then the
theologian is obligated to give an account of how
he would relate theology to other forms of knowledge.[46]
The question of how theology relates to the special
sciences (Wissenschaften) can be answered by referring
to the formal criteria of theology as discussed
above. Since theology deals with ultimate concerns,
it has no direct concern or involvement with scientific procedures or results as such. At the same
time, theology "has no right and no obligation to
prejudice a physical or historical, sociological or
psychological, inquiry."[47] Yet there is a point of
contact between science and theology, and this is
to be found in the philosophical element in both of
the disciplines. Thus the major question, that of
the relation between theology and philosophy, is
posed.

        Seeking for semantic clarity, Tillich
suggests that we define philosophy as "that
cognitive approach to reality in which reality as
such is the object."[48] This definition is offered
on the grounds that it is broad enough to cover
"most of the important philosophies which have
appeared in what is usually called the history of
philosophy," and not because it is the generally
accepted definition.[49] In another work, Tillich
defines philosophy as "that cognitive endeavor in
which the question of being is asked."[50] Philosophy,
then, deals with the question of what it means to
be, and what it means to say that something is.
Indeed, philosophy is born of the shock of such
questions as: "What is the meaning of being? Why
is there being and not not-being? What is the
structure in which every being participates?"[51]
This means that, centrally, philosophy involves
ontology. Philosophy asks the question of being;
while ontology is the word (logos) of being (on),
"the word which grasps being, makes its nature
manifest, drives it out of its hiddenness into
the light of knowledge."[52] Philosophy's task is

to separate from the many aspects of experience itself, those structures which make experience possible. Philosophy proceeds by "inquiring into the nature of reality as such," which means inquiring into "those structures, categories, and concepts which are presupposed in the cognitive encounter with every realm of reality."[53] While Tillich recognizes that there are some attempts at philosophy which seek to eliminate this ontological aspect, he feels that all these attempts will inevitably fail either because they make philosophy irrelevant or because their approach involves some implicit ontological assumptions which must finally be recognized. Philosophy necessarily involves ontology. "One cannot escape ontology if one wants to know! For knowing means recognizing something as being."[54]

If philosophy necessarily asks the question of the structure of being, theology must also ask the same question. At this point philosophy and theology share a concern. If theology deals with ultimate concern it must, of necessity, deal with that which belongs to being, for if our ultimate concern did not belong to being we could not encounter it and it would not and could not concern us.

> Of course, it cannot be one being among others; then it would not concern us infinitely. It must be the ground of our being, that which determines our being or not-being, the ultimate and unconditional power of being. But the power of being, its infinite ground or "being-itself," expresses itself in and through the structure of being. Therefore, we can encounter it, be grasped by it, know it, and act toward it. Theology, when dealing with our ultimate concern, presupposes in every sentence the structure of being, its categories, laws, and concepts.[55]

Consequently, any attempt on the part of biblicism to avoid ontological terms and problems is doomed to failure just as surely as any corresponding philosophical attempt. Even the Bible "uses the

38

categories and concepts which describe the structure of experience." Biblicism is forced to use terms that have been shaped for centuries by philosophical understandings (such as "history"); it cannot, therefore, assume the availability of a purely religious language or language unconditioned by philosophic traditions.[56]

With this admittedly hasty aside on Tillich's understanding of philosophy, we turn now to that which is to be the focus of this chapter-- the method of correlation.[57]

To speak of theology as "systematic" or to speak of a theological "method" implies that such theology has a rational character in its own right. While Tillich feels that the problem of the "rational character of theology must remain unsolved," he does indicate that some "directing principles" can be stated.[58] There must be an element of "semantic rationality," meaning that the theologian must seek for clarity and "existential purity" in his language. Special care must be taken regarding the connotations of words so that such connotations center around a controlling meaning. There being no "revealed language"--not even biblical language-- the theologian must choose those words which are deemed to be most helpful in his task. At the same time the theologian must recognize the danger of distorting the Christian message by the intrusion of "anti-Christian ideas in the cloak of a philosophical, scientific, or poetic terminology."

Theology also is characterized by a logical rationality, which implies that theology "is as dependent on formal logic as any other science."[59] Formal logic, in the sense of keeping clear of logical contradictions, as well as the affirmations and negations of dialectics both have their place in theology. The element of paradox in theology (as in Luther's formula, simul justus et peccator) is not a matter of logical contradiction, but a means of expressing the conviction that "God's acting transcends all possible human expectations

39

and all necessary human preparations. It transcends,
but it does not destroy, finite reason."[60]

       Finally, theology has a "methodological
rationality." By this Tillich seems to mean that a
theology has a consistent way of coming at its material, of deriving and stating its propositions.
Not that he expects a system which has neither gaps
nor contradictions, rather he calls for an attempt
to bring consistency of thought into theological
thinking. Life, indeed, may break through such a
systematic shell, yet there is no inherent virtue
in inconsistency as such.[61] The method of correlation attempts to abide by this rational character
of the theological enterprise. The goal is not the
production of a deductive system, since this would
be in contradiction to the existential character of
Christian truth, but to express the Christian faith
in a series of consistent assertions.

       Tillich defines the Method, itself, func-
tionally: "The method of correlation explains the
contents of the Christian faith through existential
questions and theological answers in mutual interdependence."[62] Let us attempt to elaborate the
meaning of this statement by exploring the various
key elements within it. Tillich maintains that
"correlation" can have three meanings as applied
to theological method.[63] There is, first of all,
the "correspondence" sense of correlation such as
that found between religious symbols and those
truths portrayed by or pointed to by the symbols.
The cross, for example, as a symbol in Christian
thinking, has a content of meaning which corresponds
to the cross as symbol. The cross and its meaning
"correspond." There is a "logical" sense of
correlation between "concepts denoting the human
and those denoting the divine." Tillich cites the
correlation of the infinite and the finite as an
example of this logical sense. The concepts of
finitude and infinity depend upon each other to
sustain their meaning. I gather Tillich wishes to
say that there is some inherent link between God's
nature and man's nature that allows for some

logical inter-connection of the concepts of these natures. This points to the _analogia entis_ which, Tillich asserts in another context, "gives us our only justification for speaking at all about God."[64]

The final sense of correlation is the "factual" sense "between man's ultimate concern and that about which he is ultimately concerned."[65] This seems to mean that God, as the _object_ of man's ultimate concern manifests himself, makes himself real to man, through man's own subjective involvement in ultimate concern. The divine-human relationship as exemplified in religious experience always involves the realities of the objective and subjective in strict interdependence. The objective fact of the divine becomes real for man only through the subjective fact of man's own ultimate concern. Indeed, Tillich feels that any talking about the objective side as an isolated and quasi-scientific assertion is an indication of disintegration in theology.[66] This aspect of correlation implies that no meaningful concept of God is possible without man's own subjective involvement, indeed man can know God only through man's own experience. This third meaning of correlation "qualifies the divine-human relationship within religious experience."[67]

Tillich would defend himself against the charge that this third type of correlation makes God dependent upon man. Against this charge Tillich would assert that God "in his abysmal nature" is in no way dependent upon man, but God is dependent on man in the sense that God must adjust his self-manifestation to "fit" the way in which man as man can receive such a manifestation.[68] God comes to man and makes himself real to man _through_ human channels; the divine "message" is designed to conform to and confirm the structures of human beingness. This assertion lies at the heart of Tillich's theological method, and it carries a multitude of implications regarding the nature of man, the nature of the God-man relationship, and the entire field of the role of reason

41

and revelation in the Christian understanding of
man.

The "condescending" nature of God's self-
manifestation implied in correlation is quite
clearly indicated in the cognitive side of the
divine-human relationship. Man's questions are
answered; man's questions are taken seriously;
and man's questions are the objects toward which
revelation, God's answers, are addressed. In an
observation virtually loaded with overtones for our
consideration, Tillich writes:

> Symbolically speaking, God answers man's
> questions, and under the impact of God's
> answers man asks them. Theology formulates
> the questions implied in human existence, and
> theology formulates the answers implied in
> divine self-manifestation under the guidance
> of the questions implied in human existence.[69]

Before expanding on the "questions" and
"answers" involved in the Method, let us first
consider by way of contrast three other methods
which Tillich considers to be inadequate. The
method of "supranaturalism" is inadequate since it
considers the "Christian message to be a sum of
revealed truths which have fallen into the human
situation like strange bodies from a strange world."[70]
In this method there is no correlation since the
revealed truths have no necessary relation to man's
questions as man or even man's nature as existing
man. The truths that are "thrown" into the world
must create a new situation before man can receive
them. "Man must become something else than human
in order to receive" the divine self-manifestation.
Tillich feels this method reflects docetic-mono-
physitic traits, and that it tends to look upon
the Bible as a book of supranatural "oracles" which
has no necessary relation to man's structures of
receptivity. The supranaturalistic method fails
because it assumes that man can receive meaningful
answers to questions he, as man, has never asked.

A second inadequate method may be called
the "naturalistic" or "humanistic."[71] In this

42

method, everything is said by man; both the questions
and the answers are from man, nothing is said to
man. Not only does this method seek to derive the
questions from human existence, but it also looks
to human existence for the answers. In this sense
much of liberal theology of the last two centuries
was "humanistic" and "unaware that human existence
itself is the question." Put in another way, Tillich
maintains that this view tends to identify man's
existential state with his essential state, thus
"overlooking the break between them which is reflected in the universal human condition of self-estrangement and self-contradiction."

The third method to be rejected is the "dualistic" method which seeks to build a supranatural
structure on a natural substructure.[72] Tillich does
feel that this method is aware, at least, of the
problem which his Method tries to meet. "It realizes
that, in spite of the infinite gap between man's
spirit and God's spirit, there must be a positive
relation between them." The dualistic method seeks
to express this relation by holding that there is a
body of theological truth which man, by his own
efforts, can reach. The usual name for this aspect
of theological knowledge is "natural theology"--a
term which Tillich considers to be "self-contradictory."[73] This method is true insofar as it deals
with questions implied in human finitude, but it is
false insofar as it seeks to derive the answers from
the form of the questions themselves.[74]

In contrast to the three methods just outlined, Tillich's Method is built around the assertion that meaningful and saving answers come to man
from the Divine, yet these answers are directed to
questions which in some sense come out of man himself. Since the questions are thus logically and
experientially prior to the answers, theology's
first task is to formulate the questions. But what
are these questions which are "implied in human
existence" and which "theology formulates"? Tillich
feels these questions are derived from and grow out
of man's own experience, and that these questions

43

can be formulated by man as he reflects on his experience. They are the questions which have been asked and always will be asked because man is what he is; they are the "basic questions" which were formulated in the ancient mythological materials of history. They are the questions that have been raised because men experience the "shock of transitoriness, the anxiety in which they are aware of their finitude, the threat of nonbeing."[75] To be human means to ask "the questions of one's own being."

The analysis of existence which produces the questions is a "philosophical task, even if it is done by a theologian;" yet the analysis employs materials that come from a number of cultural expressions whereby man has produced creative self-interpretation. Poetry, literature, psychology, sociology, art, and philosophy all contribute materials for such an analysis. These areas become windows through which the existential questions are seen and fields from which the questions are mined. The theologian, working as a philosopher, uses all these materials in his analysis, yet as a theologian he also keeps his eyes "partially focused" on the ultimate concern which has grasped him. This means that the Christian theologian cannot help but see human existence "in such a way that the Christian symbols appear meaningful to him;" yet in this process the theologian, as theologian, does not tell himself what is philosophically true, and the theologian, as philosopher, does not tell himself what is theologically true.[76]

If the questions, then, are drawn out of an analysis of the range of man's experience, what of the "answers"? "The Christian message provides the answers to the questions implied in human existence."[77] These answers come, not by way of informational statements, but by way of events. These are the events which contain in themselves the answers. Systematic theology formulates the answers which are contained in these revelatory events by working from the sources (the Bible, church history, and the history of religion and culture), through

the _medium_ of theology (experience), and _under_ the
norm of Christian theology (the "New Being in Jesus
as the Christ").[78] While these answers are answers
to the questions raised in the analysis of the human
situation, yet the content of the answers is not
derived from the questions themselves. The _content_
is fixed by the Christian message in its universal
validity, and these answers are "spoken" to human
existence from "beyond it." On the other hand, the
form of the answer _does_ depend upon the structure
of the question which it answers. Let us briefly
outline this "question-answer" structure as Tillich
develops it in the five sections of his theology,
then we shall suggest how questions and answers are
related in terms of form and content.

        Although Tillich asserts that theology "is
first of all doctrine of God," the first part of
Systematic Theology is a consideration of "Reason
and Revelation"--this because the epistemological
stance needs to be shown so that the basis of various
assertions can be ascertained.[79] In this first part,
then, Tillich develops the "questions" through an
analysis of man's rationality. After developing the
"structure" of reason through ontological analysis,
Tillich concludes that reason faces certain fundamental problems under the conditions of existence.
Actual reason participates in the characteristics
of reality, which means that it is involved in
finitude, in self-destructive conflicts, in ambiguities, and thus is involved in a search for a "saving" answer to such finitude, conflicts, and ambiguities.[80] As finite, reason is bound by the "categories of experience" since these are also "categories
of finitude." Reason is bounded by time, causality,
space, substance, and cannot reach the eternal, the
first cause, absolute space, and universal substance.[81]
The "questions" to be raised, then, about reason
under the conditions of existence take the form of
various problematic situations in which reason finds
itself. Tillich sums up these problematic situations
as types of conflicts:

        The polarity of structure and depth within
        reason produces a conflict between autonomous

and heteronomos reason under the conditions
of existence. Out of this conflict arises the
quest for theonomy. The polarity of the static
and the dynamic elements of reason produces a
conflict between absolutism and relativism of
reason under the conditions of existence.
This conflict leads to the quest for the
concrete-absolute. The polarity of the formal
and the emotional elements of reason produces
the conflict between formalism and irrationalism
of reason under the conditions of existence.
Out of this conflict arises the quest for the
union of form and mystery. In all three cases
reason is driven to the quest for revelation.[82]

With such "questions" (i.e., conflicts which
bring the quest for revelation) posed by way of a
philosophical analysis of reason in existence,
Tillich then brings the other pole of the Method to
bear by showing how Christian revelation answers
the questions thus posed. After a lengthy description of the meaning of revelation and its actuality,
Tillich shows how the final revelation in Jesus as
the Christ overcomes the conflicts of reason in
existence ("saves" or "heals" reason). "Final revelation does not destroy reason; it fulfills reason.
It liberates reason from" the various conflicts.[83]
Reason is liberated from the conflict between heteronomy and autonomy by finding a basis for theonomous
reason--where autonomous reason is united with its
depth so that neither heteronomy nor autonomy pre-
vail, but theonomy. The "essential unity" between
heteronomy and autonomy is re-established by the
final revelation in Jesus as the Christ, since this
revelation is "completely transparent" to the
"ground of being" thereby establishing the element
of the "depth" of being; and this revelatory event,
through the complete self-sacrifice of the medium
of revelation, undercuts any heteronomous claim that
may be made by the finite medium.[84]

The final revelation liberates reason from
the conflict between absolutism and relativism by
"appearing in the form of a concrete absolute."

46

The final revelation came by way of a personal life, "the most concrete of all possible forms of concreteness,"[85] Yet this personal life is absolute since he is seen as the bearer of "that which is absolute without condition and restriction." He is the logos, the self-manifestation of God, made flesh. Finally, revelation heals reason by overcoming the conflict between formalism and irrationalism.[86] This conflict is overcome since the totality of a person's life participates in the revelatory experience, thus the rational and the emotional aspects of personhood participate in the experience and are, in a sense, brought into harmony. Technical reason, the element of detachment, is not destroyed, but it is balanced by a "uniting knowledge" which sustains meaning and the mystery of being.

Having spelled out in some detail the first part of the system, we shall summarize more briefly the correlative aspects of the other four parts. Part II, "Being and God," begins with an analysis of man's beingness as characterized by human finitude. The "question" raised by the problematic nature of finitude is the quest for or the question of God. Christian theology "answers" such a question by asserting the reality of God and by spelling out the meaning of God by way of the "symbols which constitute the idea of God."[87] Part III, "Existence and the Christ," deals with an analysis of the existential disruption and despair found in human existence. The answer to the question of the healing of this disruption and despair is found in the "symbol of the Christ and his appearance under the conditions of existence."[88] Part IV of Systematic Theology, "Life and the Spirit," deals with an analysis of the ambiguities of life experienced as a mixture of essential and existential being.[89] The "answer" to these tragic ambiguities is to be found in the uniting function of the divine spirit. Since the ambiguities of life are never totally overcome within historical existence, the question of the meaning of history and its goal is posed in part V, "History and the Kingdom of God." The answer to the questions involved in that dimension of life which we call history is to be found in and developed from the

47

symbol of the Kingdom of God.[90]

With this overview of the various parts of
the system, indicating how "question" and "answer"
are correlated, we shall turn back to a consideration
of what Tillich means when he states that the "content"
of the answer is fixed by the Christian message,
while the "form" of the answer is determined by the
"form" of the question to which it is addressed.
In Tillich's words, "In respect to content the
Christian answers are dependent on the revelatory
events in which they appear; in respect to form they
are dependent on the structure of the questions
which they answer."[91] By "form" of the question,
Tillich seems to mean the subject matter of the
question, the specific problem areas of existence
as they are developed through philosophical analysis.
Certainly Tillich does not mean, by "form," the
linguistic or logical structure of the questions.
Thus the "form" of the questions involves such matters
as the conflicts in reason, human finitude, existential disruption and estrangement, the ambiguities
of life, and the meaning of historical existence
and history in general. This form--I suggest "subject matter" as an alternative phrasing--of the
question is fixed by the philosophical side of
correlation. Thus when the theological "answer" is
given, it must answer in terms of the nature of the
questions raised, in terms of the subject matter
developed by the analysis. But the answer, while
true to the "form" of the question, brings the
"content" of the Christian message to bear. The
specific symbols of the revelatory events are
related directly to and interpreted in conjunction
with the questions in their form. Thus Christian
theology brings the "answers" of: revelation, the
idea of God, Jesus as the Christ, the divine Spirit,
and the Kingdom of God.

This interpretation of the form-content
relation would seem to be consistent with Tillich's
statement of the matter in another work. "The
questions implied in human existence determine the
meaning of the theological interpretation of the
answers as they appear in the classical religious

48

concepts."[92] While this is a very bold statement
of the relation, still it reflects the idea that the
"subject-matter" of the question and answer, as its
"meaning," is controlled by the nature of the questions
themselves. Perhaps even a thorough-going Tillichian
may be a bit uneasy about this intimate linkage
between the question and answer. Small wonder that
theologians of the Barthian stripe raise the question
of the danger to God's sovereign freedom implied in
the Method.[93]

It must be said at this point, however, that
Tillich, true to his general style, has no simplistic
view of the form-content distinction. Since there
is an interrelatedness between the questions and
answers themselves, there can be no sharp distinction
between the form and content of the answers for the
Christian theologian. Indeed, this distinction itself becomes blurred in the following section:

> The form of the questions, whether primitive
> or philosophical, is decisive for the theolog-
> ical form in which the answer is given. And,
> conversely, the substance of the question is
> determined by the substance of the answer. No-
> body is able to ask questions concerning God,
> revelation, Christ, etc., who has not already
> received some answer. So we can say: With
> respect to man's ultimate concern the questions
> contain the substance of the answers, and the
> answers are shaped by the form of the questions.
> Here the rational element in theological method
> has a determining influence on theological
> propositions--not on their substance but on
> their form. But there is no way of saying a
> priori how much substance is hidden in the
> form. This can be said only in the process of
> theological work, and never fully.[94]

In this context, let us recall a quotation where
Tillich indicates that the distinction between the
nature of the existential questions raised and the
theological answers given is also somewhat overcome:
"Symbolically speaking, God answers man's questions,

and under the impact of God's answers man asks them"[95]

It is tempting to suggest that Tillich's mind
begins to take on the characteristics of Nicolaus
of Cusa's idea of God as the <u>coincidentia oppositorum</u>.[96]
Nor is this suggestion intended to be only a gibe,
since it is clear that Cusanus is one of several
theologians who have made their impact on Tillich's
thought. Both in terms of method and in terms of
his own ontological vision Tillich would assert
that while polarities may exist within reality and
thought, the interrelatedness of the whole of reality
overcomes any final distinction or cleavage. As
part of actual reason, then, Tillich's mind should
indeed not only reflect the distinctions in the
structure of being, but should also be able to
engulf them in a greater unity! Regarding the
Method Tillich has commented:

> I fully agree . . . that no "nice division"
> between existentialist questions and theological
> answers is possible . . . because the nature of
> the method itself makes this impossible. Questions
> and answers determine each other in a definable
> way. And in the case of the theologian, both
> lie within the "theological circle" which is
> characterized by this interdependence.[97]

From the standpoint of ontology, the following
quotation carries the flavor of Tillich's vision
of the pluralism of elements within the unity of
reality:

> One cannot deny that being is one and that
> the qualities and elements of being constitute
> a texture of connected and conflicting forces.
> This texture is one, insofar as it <u>is</u> and gives
> the power of being to each of its qualities
> and elements. . . . It is one in the manifold-
> ness of its texture. Ontology is the attempt
> to describe this texture, to reveal its hidden
> nature through the word which belongs to being
> and in which being comes to itself.[98]

50

In another statement where he ties the Method to his ontological "vision" (as I have called it), Tillich asserts:

> This mixture of mutual dependence on, and independence of, question and answer characterizes all life processes. It is not a unique theological phenomenon and is not restricted to what I call the "method of correlation."[99]

Needless to say, Tillich's theology would be the despair of anyone who seeks for a tight logical system with neatly defined, deductive, and transparent elements; nor would he warm the hearts of those who desire conclusive methods of verification. But in being honest with life, as he has come to experience it and understand it, Tillich opts for an approach that is suggestive in its breadth and depth.

Tillich has dedicated the first volume of his Systematic Theology to his students both in Germany and in the United States. He states that he hopes these students will find in his works "a help in answering the questions they are asked by people inside and outside their churches. A help in answering questions: this is exactly the purpose of this theological system."[100] In offering his philosophical theology and his Method as a "help" Tillich does not assert that either his theology or his Method has some kind of final validity which can be ascertained from totally objective considerations. He does, to be sure, feel that his is a fruitful Method and system through which one can attack the "two centuries' old question of 'Christianity and the modern mind' with some success.[101] Yet the Method is itself a "theological assertion,and, like all theological assertions, it is made with passion and risk."[102] Which, of course, means that we have returned to the "theological circle" in which any theologian works. Paul Johannes Tillich wrote his theological works out of the circle in which he found himself hoping that through his writings others would see more clearly the nature of their questions and perhaps also discover that they are grasped by the Christian message. This is the final aim of the Method.

FOOTNOTES

1. For some examples of "non-participating" admiration see: Reinhold Niebuhr, "Biblical Thought and Ontological Speculation," The Theology of Paul Tillich, ed. Kegley and Bretall (New York: The Macmillan Co., 1956), pp. 226-227; and Kenneth Hamilton, The System and the Gospel (New York: The Macmillan Co., 1963), pp. 9-10.

For some account of the sources of Tillich's complexity and richness see the following: Wilhelm Pauck, "The Sources of Paul Tillich's Richness," Union Seminary Quarterly Review, Vol. XXI (November, 1965), pp. 3-9; Paul Tillich, "Autobiographical Reflections," in Kegley and Bretall, op. cit., pp. 3-21; A. J. McKelway, The Systematic Theology of Paul Tillich (Richmond: John Knox Press, 1964), pp. 17-35; and see Tillich's development of his own "boundary line" stance in his The Interpretation of History (New York: Charles Scribner's Sons, 1936).

2. For the sake of brevity we shall use the capitalized "Method" to refer to the method of correlation throughout this work.

3. Paul Tillich, The Eternal Now (Scribner paperback; New York: Charles Scribner's Sons, 1963), p. 112.

4. Paul Tillich, Systematic Theology (3 vols., Chicago: University of Chicago Press, 1951-1963), Vol. I, p. 145, and Vol. II, p. 166. Hereafter this work will be cited as S.T., followed by volume number in Roman numerals and page number in Arabic numerals.

5. S.T., II, 166.
6. Tillich, The Eternal Now, p. 113.
7. S.T., II, 165.
8. S.T., I, 11.
9. D. Mackenzie Brown, Ultimate Concern: Tillich in Dialogue (New York: Harper and Row, 1965), pp. 7, 8 and 20.
10. Paul Tillich, Christianity and the Encounter With the World Religions (Columbia paperback; New York: Columbia University Press, 1964), p. 4.
11. S.T., I, 12.
12. S.T., I, 13. Tillich points out that this

53

description has some negative implications for the
work of a tholoogian. He insists that the theologian
as theologian is no expert in any matters of preliminary concerns. "Theology cannot and should not
give judgments about the aesthetic value of an
artistic creation, about the scientific value of a
physical theory or a historical conjecture, about
the best methods of medical healing or social
reconstruction, about the solution of political or
international conflicts." (S.T., I, 12.) The
theologian, then, should not and need not feel
anxious about his ability to speak some kind of
definitive word in every situation.
    13. Brown, Ultimate Concern. . ., p. 11. Tillich
insists that his phrase "ultimate concern" is not
designed to replace the traditional term "God."
    14. Ibid., p. 21-22. Tillich has obvious
affinities with Schleiermacher at this point. For
a neat contrast of Schleiermacher as against Barth,
Brunner, and Bonhoeffer see Richard R. Niebuhr,
Schleiermacher on Christ and Religion (Scribner
paperback; New York: Charles Scribner's Sons, 1964),
pp. 174 ff.
    15. Paul Tillich, The Dynamics of Faith (Harper
paperback; New York: Harper and Brothers, 1958),
pp. 1, 8 and 32.
    16. Paul Tillich, Biblical Religion and the
Search for Ultimate Reality (Chicago: The University
of Chicago Press, 1956), p. 51.
    17. Tillich, The Dynamics . . ., p. 30.
Tillich develops the common distortions of faith
in the pages which follow.
    18. For an illustration of this problem in
Protestant history, see Jeraslov Pelikan, From
Luther to Kierkegaard (Paperback; Saint Louis:
Concordia Publishing House, 1963), pp. 28, 59-61.
    19. Tillich, Dynamics. . ., pp. 35 ff.
    20. Ibid., p. 39.
    21. Paul Tillich, The Protestant Era (Phoenix
Books; Chicago: University of Chicago Press, 1957),
p. x.
    22. Tillich, Biblical Religion . . ., pp.
60-61.
    23. Tillich, Dynamics . . ., pp. 17-18.
There are some interesting parallels with Martin
Heidegger at this point. ". . . a faith that does

not perpetually expose itself to the possibility
of unfaith is no faith but merely a convenience:
the believer simply makes up his mind to adhere
to the traditional doctrine. /Cf. Tillich's
"intellectualistic" and "voluntaristic" distortions
of faith./ This is neither faith nor questioning,
but the indifference of those who can busy themselves with everything, sometimes even displaying
a keen interest in faith as well as questioning."
This is from his An Introduction to Metaphysics,
trans. Ralph Manehim (Anchor Books; Garden City:
Doubleday and Co., Inc., 1961), p. 6.

24. Brown, Ultimate Concern . . ., p. 9.

25. Ibid., p. 11. Just before these statements, Tillich quotes with approval Luther's
comment, "Man is like a horse which is ridden by
a rider; it is either God or the devil."

26. For a discussion of the "quasi-religions"
see Tillich, Christianity and the Encounter . . .,
p. 4 ff. Note, also, that on the basis of this
understanding of religion, a passionate atheism
is logically impossible. "Where there is ultimate
concern, God can be denied only in the name of God."
Tillich, Dynamics . . ., p. 5.

27. See Brown, Ultimate Concern . . ., pp. 50-
51. At this point we must mention the striking
parallel between Tillich and Luther in this matter.
In his Large Catechism Luther writes, "A God is
that to which we look for all good and in which we
find refuge in every time of need. . . . As I have
often said, the trust and faith of the heart alone
make both God and idol. . . . That to which your
heart clings and entrusts itself is, I say, really
your God. . . . Many a person thinks he has God
and everything he needs when he has money and
property; in them he trusts and of them he boasts
so stubbornly and securely that he cares for no one.
Surely such a man also has a god--mammon by name,
that is, money and possessions--on which he fixes
his whole heart." From Martin Luther, The Large
Catechism, R. H. Fisher, trans. (Philadelphia,
Fortress Press, 1959), p. 9. Compare Tillich's
comment: ". . . whatever concerns a man ultimately
becomes god for him, and, conversely, . . . a man
can be concerned ultimately only about that which

is god for him.: (S.T., I, 211.)

28. Tillich, Dynamics . . ., pp. 126-127.
29. S.T., I, 3.
30. S.T., I, 3-4. Tillich explains that by "situation" he means the "scientific and artistic, the economic, political, and ethical forms in which they /individuals and groups/ express their interpretation of existence." Thus "situation" does not refer to the particular psychological or sociological state in which persons find themselves.
31. S.T., I, 5.
32. S.T., I, 6.
33. S.T., I, 6-7.
34. S.T., I, 8.
35. S.T., I, 9.
36. A more complete elaboration of this line of thinking must wait until Chapter V.
37. See S.T., I, 11-15, for Tillich's development of the formal criteria.
38. S.T., I, 11.
39. S.T., I, 12.
40. S.T., I, 14.
41. S.T., I, 14.
42. S.T., I, 15.
43. S.T., I, 16.
44. S.T., I, 15.
45. S.T., I, 16-17. In two pages of somewhat abstruse reasoning, Tillich seeks to show that Christian theology is, in fact, the theology because it combines in a unique way these principles of universality and concreteness. He ends the section with this observation: "It is obvious that these arguments do not prove the assertion of faith that in Jesus the Logos has become flesh. But they show that, if this assertion is accepted, Christian theology has a foundation which infinitely transcends the foundations of everything in the history of religion which could be called 'theology.'" (S.T., I, 18, underlining mine). One is tempted to ask what has been gained through this argument. After all, the argument has its final weight only if the claim that Jesus Christ is the Logos become flesh is accepted; yet it is precisely this claim that is an assertion of faith! And if this assertion is made by faith certainly the argument itself is not needed.

46. S.T., I, 18.
47. S.T., I, 18.
48. S.T., I, 18. In the words of John Herman Randall, Jr., "Tillich is clearly not a Cambridge analyst." For an interesting account of G. E. Moore's reaction to a presentation by Tillich see John Herman Randall,Jr., "The Ontology of Paul Tillich," Kegley and Bretall, op. cit., p. 133. While appreciating Moore's point, Randall observes nicely, "The precise statement of nothing of consequence is surely specious, and the meaning of human destiny can scarcely be cramped within the bounds of symbolic logic."

49. Tillich grants that there is, in fact, no generally accepted definition of philosophy. He goes on to imply that the philosopher, himself, moves within a circle even in the definition he would give to philosophy. "Every philosopher proposes a definition which agrees with the interest, purpose, and method of the philosopher." (S.T., I, 18.) This "circle" is defined by the presuppositions which the philosopher accepts in order to do his philosophizing. The presupposition which shapes the circle in which Tillich would philosophize is "that there is an identity, or at least an analogy, between objective and subjective reason, between the logos of reality as a whole and the logos working in him . . . this logos is in common; every reasonable being participates in it . . ." (S.T., I, 23.)

50. Tillich, Biblical Religion . . ., p. 5.
51. Tillich, The Protestant Era, p. 85.
52. Tillich, Biblical Religion . . ., p. 6. For some sections which develop his view of philosophy see: S.T., I, 18 ff.; Biblical Religion . . ., pp. 5 ff.; Paul Tillich, Love, Power, and Justice (New York, Oxford Univerity Press, 1954), pp. 18 ff.

53. S.T., I, 18. Tillich goes on to say that this "critical definition" of philosophy results in a philosophic enterprise that is "more modest" than those which seek to present a complete system of reality, such as Hegel. Yet this understanding of philosophy is "less modest" than those which attempt to reduce philosophy to epistemology and ethics or to logical calculus, such as the Neo-Kantians and the logical positivists.

54. Tillich, _Love_, _Power_ . . ., pp. 19-20.
See also S.T., I, 20.
55. S.T., I, 21.
56. In his _Biblical_ _Religion_ . . ., Tillich
seeks to spell out in detail the necessary link
between biblical thought and ontology.
57. In Chapter V we must wrestle at some
length with Tillich's understanding of the distinction between philosophy and theology, and the nature
of reason and its role in the Method.
58. S.T., I, 54 ff. A development of reason
in its "formal" and "ecstatic" elements must wait
until Chapter V.
59. S.T., I, 56.
60. S.T., I, 57.
61. Tillich shrewdly points out that some of
the most passionate foes of the system are, themselves, quite thoroughly "systematic" in their
utterances. See S.T., I, 58.
62. S.T., I, 60.
63. S.T., I, 57.
64. S.T., I, 240.
65. S.T., I, 60.
66. Paul Tillich, "The Problem of Theological
Method," _Four_ _Existentialist_ _Theologians_, ed. Will
Herberg (Garden City: Doubleday and Co., Inc.,
1958), p. 279.
67. S.T., I, 61.
.68. S.T., I, 61. This implication is carried
over into Tillich's understanding of the Incarnation.
(S.T., II, 94-95.) This aspect of correlation has
much in common with Luther's understanding of the
"theology of the cross." Cf. Pinomaa, op. cit,
pp. 3-11. On page eleven Pinomaa writes of Luther's
theology, "The revelation of God can reach us only
within the bounds of our human limitations and
imperfections."
69. S.T., I, 61.
70. S.T., I, 64.
71. S.T., I, 65.
72. S.T., I, 65.
73. Tillich, "The Problem of Theological
Method," pp. 277-278; Paul Tillich, "What is Wrong
with 'Dialectic' Theology," _The_ _Journal_ _of_ _Religion_,

Vol. XV (April, 1935), p. 140; and S.T., I, 65.

74. Tillich asserts that all the "so-called" arguments for the "existence of God" (another self-contradictory term) fall into this error of the dualistic method. Cf. S.T., I, 204 ff.

75. S.T., I, 62. The content and form of the specific questions will be illustrated and discussed in the latter part of this chapter.

76. S.T., I, 63. This relation between theologian as philosopher and as theologian will be clarified, hopefully, in Chapter V when we shall explore more precisely those elements involved in the asking of the questions.

77. S.T., I, 64.

78. See S.T., I, 34 ff., for Tillich's development of the sources, medium, and norm.

79. S.T., I, 67. But Tillich insists that "it is an error to assume that epistemology is able to provide the foundation of the philosophical or theological system." While the epistemological section may precede other parts it is dependent on the other parts since "every epistemological assertion is implicitly ontological." (S.T., I, 71).

80. S.T., I, 81.

81. S.T., I, 82. Tillich asserts that both Nicolaus Cusanus and Immanuel Kant deftly describe this finitude of reason--Cusanus through his "docta ignorantia", Kant through his doctrine of the categories.

82. S.T., I, 83.

83. S.T., I, 150.

84. S.T., I, 147-148. Admittedly this is a brief and, therefore, somewhat indistinct summary of a lengthy and stimulating section of the systematics.

85. S.T., I, 150.

86. S.T., I, 153 ff.

87. Tillich, "The Problem of . . .," p. 279. The entire systematic development of this part is found in S.T., I, 161-289.

88. Tillich, "The Problem of . . .," p. 280. The entire second volume of Systematic Theology deals with this part of his system.

89. This part of the system is found in S.T., III, 11-294.

90. Part V, the final part of the system, is developed in S.T., III, 297-423.

91. S.T., I, 64. (Underlining mine).

92. Tillich, "The Problem of . . .," p. 280. Underlining is mine.

93. For a discussion of this problem from the standpoint of a general Barthian pose, see McKelway, op. cit., pp. 67-70. I would submit that McKelway misunderstands what Tillich means by this form-content distinction when he writes, "But if the divine Logos took this form /becoming flesh/, then how can this form be said to have been determined by the questions of men if it is the true paradoxa . . ." (Underlining is mine.) The ambiguity of "form" misled McKelway at this point. Surely Tillich maintains that the "Logos become flesh" is part of the unchanging content of the Christian message, and is not at all dependent on the form of the questions as we have tried to spell this out above.

94. Tillich, "The Problem of . . .," p. 280. (Underlining is mine.)

95. S.T., I, 61.

96. Copleston describes this coincidentia oppositorum as "the synthesis of opposites, which transcends and yet includes the distinct perfections of creatures." See F. Copleston, S.J., A History of Philosophy (7 vols.; Image Books; Garden City: Doubleday and Co., Inc., 1963), Vol. 3, Part II, p. 39.

97. In Sydney and Beatrice Rome, Philosophical Interrogations (New York: Holt, Rinehart and Winston, 1964), p. 372.

98. Tillich, Love, Power and Justice, pp. 19-20.

99. Rome, op. cit., p. 362.

100. S.T., I, viii.

101. S.T., I, 8. Note that in his Biblical Religion . . ., p. 85, Tillich insists that there "is no saving ontology" nor is there any special ontology that must be accepted in the name of the biblical message.

102. S.T., I, 8.

CHAPTER III

SUGGESTED PARALLELS AND PROBLEMS

On the face of it, the proposal that there
are parallels between Martin Luther's Law-Gospel
distinction and Paul Tillich's method of Correlation
smacks either of superficial associationism or a
bald attempt at enunciating shocking statements.
After all, if one can ask, in Tertullian's famous
phrase, "What has Athens to do with Jerusalem?",
surely one can question any fundamental relationship between Luther and Tillich. Anyone who is
theologically literate knows of Luther's tirades
against "madame reason," and would see the bold
contrast in Tillich's love for and bold espousal
of the role of philosophy. How can a Luther who
spoke disparagingly of philosophy and "the philosopher" be linked essentially to a Tillich whose
thinking is virtually saturated with philosophy
that dates from the Pre-Socratics to Heidegger?
How can a theologian who writes with the clarity
of simplicity, using biblical and classical
Christian terminology, be tied to a theologian
whose prose often baffles the common reader and
who seems to avoid biblical language like the
plague? Are we not venturing into a theological
cul-de-sac?

On the other hand our proposal comes close
to being a truism. Consider, for example, Tillich's
own background. Born and raised in a Lutheran
parsonage, Tillich was saturated with types of
Lutheran environment during most of his formative
years. Furthermore, the men who taught him and
influenced him the most theologically and philo-
sophically--Kant, Schelling, Boehme, Hegel,
Kierkegaard, Ernest Troeltsch, A. Harnack, and
Martin Kahler--were men who had roots in the
Lutheran tradition.[1] Thus it is not at all surprising, historically speaking, to find that Tillich
himself claims to be Lutheran in his origins and
stance.

I, myself, belong to Lutheranism by birth, education, religious experience, and theological reflection. I have never stood on the borders of Lutheranism and Calvinism. . . . The substance of my religion is and remains Lutheran. . . . Not only my theological, but also my philosophical thinking expresses the Lutheran substance.[2]

In the light of Tillich's own background and his self-identification, it seems strange that more has not been written tying Tillich substantially to Luther. Or perhaps the paucity of such material is only an indication that such a connection is tenuous indeed.[3] At any rate, this work is an attempt to begin exploration of an area which, I believe, warrants a good deal of attention.

While it is quite possible, I am convinced, to show considerable relationship between the contents of Luther's and Tillich's theologies, this work will concentrate on the methodological aspects of both men's thought. Without considering how our two theologians may be related in terms of classical Christian doctrines, this dissertation will argue that Paul Tillich's method of correlation is a methodological parallel of Luther's distinction between Law and Gospel. In arguing this line we must show not only structural similarities, but we must also show that certain key assumptions underlie both methods.[4] Given the central importance of the Law-Gospel distinction in Luther's theology and the Method in Tillich's, it would seem fair to assert that these approaches must be basically compatible if Tillich's claim to be a Lutheran theologian is to be upheld.

Put in its simplest terms, we shall seek to show that when Tillich develops the existential questions and then shows how the Christian message answers these questions he is doing essentially what Luther does when he preaches the Law and then brings the Gospel to bear as the remedy for man's bondage under the Law. In its primary or theolog-

62

ical use, we have seen, Luther asserts that the Law
shows man his need of grace and drives him to the
Gospel, to Christ. "Those who are well have no
need for a physician, but those who are sick; . . ."[5]
Even so Tillich, as he elaborates the questions,
seeks to show the brokenness and the problematic
nature of human existence. He feels that man's
existential situation must be clarified before the
Christian answers can be applied; " . . . man cannot receive answers to questions he has never
asked."[6] On the other hand, Luther understands the
Gospel as the good news of God's forgiving grace
through Christ which redeems man from the burden
and condemnation of the Law. In parallel terms,
Tillich sees the healing answers as "given" to man
centrally through the Christian revelation in Jesus
as the Christ. Thus Luther's "Law" is Tillich's
"questions," while Luther's "Gospel" is Tillich's
"answers." While such an overview of the parallels
indicates certain structural similarities in method,
a thorough investigation of the details will be
needed to see if the parallels follow through in
certain key assumptions and assertions. We must
examine Tillich's Method in the light of Luther's
thinking.

The investigation to be undertaken must
show that Luther's understanding of man's relationship to and knowing of the Law has its parallels
in Tillich's understanding of man's relationship to
and knowing of the existential questions. On the
other hand, our analysis must show that Luther's
understanding of man's relationship to and knowing
of the Gospel has its parallels in Tillich's artic-
ulation of man's relationship to and knowing of
the "answers." In short, we will need to do a
substantial analysis of the role of reason and the
role of revelation in both Luther and Tillich.
The key question to pursue is: "How do these two
theologians envisage the relationship between faith
and reason?"

When we deal with Tillich's use of reason
we must be especially aware of charges from the
Barthian position regarding the adequacy and rel-

evancy of the kinds of "questions" which reason as reason can raise. Can man as man ask the right questions regarding human existence understood in the Christian perspective? Are Tillich's questions able to be understood as the Christian questions?[7] To put this charge in other terms, we will need to inquire not only if the correct questions are asked, but also if there is anything like a saving knowledge of God outside the revelation in Christ for either Tillich or Luther.

Other questions about methodology must be raised. For instance, we will want to ask whether or not any sharp distinction between Law and Gospel in Luther or between the questions and the answers in Tillich can be maintained--a question which is crucial for the understanding of the thought of both men. Furthermore, we will need to acknowledge that Tillich's system tends to subsume the central thrust of Luther's concern into a larger scheme. That is to say, Luther's focus on guilt and forgiveness--his quest for a gracious God--is but one facet of Tillich's interpretation of the human dilemma and the Christian answer.

Implied in this question of the compatibility of Tillich's Method with Luther's Law-Gospel distinction, in terms of the role of reason, is another question. Does Tillich's Method guard the godliness of God, as Luther understands such? Or, more traditionally, does Tillich's Method safeguard the central principle of Luther's theology, "justification by grace alone through faith alone?" If the Method either subverts or endangers this affirmation, then Tillich's claim to be a child of Lutheranism is certainly to be controverted.

Finally, we will want to consider whether or not Tillich might feasibly be charged, from Luther's point of view, with the presumptuous and dangerous error of a "theology of glory." This type of question is raised, indirectly, in a provocative book by John Cobb. Two quotations from Cobb's work will set the tone for this problem:

We must then recognize both that no specifically
Christian act is involved in recognizing being-
itself as God and that this means that Tillich's
idea of God is largely determined by independent
philosophical considerations.[8]
. . . .
The whole system depends upon basic philosophical
judgments which obviously are not shared by most
philosophers today. Hence, we can follow
Tillich's theology only if we first believe that
he has made his case as a philosopher.[9]

The implications of such observations are highly
important for our present study; thus we must
determine to what extent, if any, Cobb's criticisms
are valid. All this leads us, now, to Chapters IV
and V for a consideration of the role of reason in
Luther's and Tillich's theological enterprises.

FOOTNOTES

1. A conspicuous exception is F.D.E. Schleiermacher who was related to the Reformed tradition. Yet, in many ways it can be said that Schleiermacher was deeply shaped by Lutheranism and that he was very much "at home" in Lutheran environment.

2. Tillich, The Interpretation of History, p. 54.

3. The only extensive item I have yet found which attempts to describe Tillich's "Lutheran" stance is an unpublished paper by Carl Braaten entitled, "Paul Tillich As A Lutheran Theologian?" On the other hand, Jerald Brauer implies that Tillich moves away from Luther's Law-Gospel distinction on the grounds that "the distinction of the two realms is not susceptible to modern interpretation." (Brauer, op. cit., p. 23.)

4. It is interesting to note that Tillich never once mentions the "Law-Gospel" distinction in his three volumes of Systematic Theology. Nor does he mention this distinction in any of his works, to my knowledge, including his A History of Christian Thought (P.H. John, ed., an unauthorized printing of Tillich's lectures which were given at Harvard University, Cambridge, 1956), which contains a lengthy section on Luther's theology!

5. Mark 2:7.

6. S.T., I, 65.

7. Typical of such Barthian accusations is R.C. Johnson's observation on Tillich's thought: " . . . to put it baldly, there is no assurance or guarantee that the questions with which Christian theology deals are Christian questions--even less that they are the Christian questions." (Johnson, op. cit., p. 119.) McKelway presents the same criticism when he asserts that we can accept the correlations of questions and answer only ". . . if two conditions are met: if the divine answer is really God's answer and if the human questions are really man's questions." (McKelway, op. cit., p. 69.) Both Johnson and McKelway, in these very

66

helpful books, move within the "circle" of
Barthian assumptions, thus their criticisms have
their power only if one happens to be in the same
circle. In a certain sense both authors get at
crucial issues, but they beg the whole question of
theological method. In this work we shall suggest
that Tillich, while he may not agree with Barth,
would be very much at home in Luther's thought--
an observation which, to be sure, validates neither
Tillich nor Barth as such. For Barth's criticisms
of Tillich see his multi-volume Church Dogmatics,
authorized translation edited by G. W. Bromiley
and T. F. Torrance (Edinburgh: T. & T. Clark, 1936--).
Barth has eleven critical references to Tillich in
Volume I/1, published originally in German in 1932,
while there are only two other references to Tillich
in the remaining eleven volumes. For a more recent
criticism see Karl Barth, Evangelical Theology:
An Introduction, trans. Grover Foley (Anchor Books;
Garden City: Doubleday and Co., 1964), pp. 98-101.
For Barth's criticisms of and response to his
Lutheran critics see Church Dogmatics, IV/3, pp.
370-371, and his "Evangelium und Gesetz," Theol.
Existenz heute, No. 32, 1935.
    8. John B. Cobb, Living Options in Protestant
Theology (Philadelphia: The Westminster Press,
1962), p. 278.
    9. Ibid., p. 282.

CHAPTER IV

THEOLOGY AND REASON: LUTHER

Judging from their writings, it seems that a substantial number of recent and contemporary scholars feel that Luther's major sin against humanity is his disparagement of reason. Walter Kaufmann, for instance, while reflecting a certain admiration for the power of Luther's prose and the earthy nature of his profanities, recoils when Luther refers to reason as a "whore" and as the "ugly" woman who is the "devil's bride." And he finds Luther "frightening" when the Reformer writes, "Faith must trample under foot all reason, sense, and understanding, and whatever it sees it must put out of sight, and wish to know nothing but the word of God."[1] Nor do such criticisms come only from stances outside the Christian tradition. Arnold Lunn can write: Luther was "the leader of the sixteenth-century revolt not only against Rome but also against reason"; and, "Hitler's scream, 'We think with our blood' is merely a new version of Luther's description of reason as the 'devil's whore.'"[2]

Reflecting much the same point of view, Jacques Maritain, in one of his early works, writes of Luther: "He delivered men from intelligence, from that wearisome and besetting compulsion to think always and think logically."[3] And even the man whom we are considering as a son of Lutheranism can gently reprimand by writing:

. . . the Reformers combined their discovery of the existential character of theology with a badly defined rejection of reason. If it is understood that reason receives revelation and that it is an object of salvation like every other element of reality, a theology which uses theonomous reason may again be possible.[4]

What can be made of these and other charges level-
ed against Luther?[5]

It needs to be granted, at the outset, that
Luther's utterances against reason were strong indeed. The most quoted passage in this vein comes
from Luther's last sermon at Wittenberg on January
17, 1546.

But the devil's bride, reason, the lovely whore
comes in and wants to be wise, and what she
says, she thinks, is the Holy Spirit . . . for
she is the foremost whore the devil has. The
other gross sins can be seen, but nobody can
control reason. It walks about, cooks up
fanaticism (Schwarmerei) with baptism and the
Lord's Supper, and claims that everything that
pops into its head and the devil puts into
its heart is the Holy Spirit.[6]

Nor is this stance limited to the "old Luther," for
in his lectures on Paul's letter to the Romans
Luther can write:

Now it is true that everyone knows the law of
nature and that reason pleads for the best.
But what best? It pleads for that which is
best, not according to God's standards, but
according to ours, in other words: it pleads
for an evil kind of good. For it seeks itself
and its own in all things but not in God.[7]

Or consider Luther's many references to "reason"
in his lectures on Galatians (1531). Here the vast
majority of Luther's comments about reason are
either disdainful or condescending. While his
language here isn't as strong as in the sermon of
1546, the adjectives Luther ties to reason include:
blind, unspiritual, superstitious, heretical, and
idolatrous.

Seeing philosophy as a venture of human
reason, Luther can be cited as speaking disparagingly of this discipline. At one point he writes,

70

" . . . philosophy stinks in our nostrils, . . ."[8]
Later in the same work he writes:

> But, alas, how deeply and painfully we are
> caught up in categories and quiddities, and
> how many foolish opinions befog us in meta-
> physics! When shall we learn to see that we
> waste so much precious time with such useless
> studies and neglect better ones? . . . Indeed,
> I believe that I owe this duty to the Lord of
> crying out against philosophy and turning men
> to Holy Scripture.[9]

Yet on the whole, Luther's attitude toward
philosophy is never as consistently negative as his
blasts against "reason"--a point which must be
investigated later. Gerrish quotes Luther's Table-
Talk: "I do not disapprove its /philosophy's/ use,
but let us use it as a shadow, a comedy, and as
political righteousness."[10] Thus Luther would
allow philosophy to function--as long as it kept
on proper domain.

While recognizing Luther's hostile attitude
toward reason and his condescending stance toward
philosophy, we cannot conclude that such is his
sole position, for Luther's statements about reason
do not exhibit a uniform hostility, rather they
"present a strangely ambivalent attitude, alternately
heaping upon reason extravagant praise and unquali-
fied opprobrium."[11] Perhaps the most positive
statement he makes regarding reason is from a set
of theses developed in 1536:

> (4) . . . reason is the most important and the
> highest in rank among all things, and, in
> comparison with other things of this life, the
> best and something divine. (5) It is the in-
> ventor and mentor of all the arts, medicines,
> laws, and of whatever wisdom, power, virtue,
> and glory men possess in this life. (6) By
> virtue of this fact it ought to be named the
> essential difference by which man is distin-
> guished from the animals and other things. . . .
> (8) That is, that it is a sun and a kind of

71

god appointed to administer these things in this life.[12]

In another context, Luther stresses the positive role reason plays in human life:

> In temporal affairs and those which have to do with men, the rational man is self-sufficient . . . ; here he needs no other light than reason's. Therefore, God does not teach us in the Scriptures how to build houses, make clothing, marry, wage war, navigate, and the like. For here the light of nature is sufficient.[13]

In much the same way Luther can pay his compliments to the philosophers. In his lectures on Genesis, for instance, he writes:

> For those who want to learn nothing else /than to do what they ought to do/, it would be enough to provide Cato's poem or Aesop, whom I consider the better teacher of morals. Nevertheless it is profitable to put both into the hands of young people. Let the older ones learn Cicero, to whom, to my surprise, some prefer Aristotle as a teacher of morals. This is, in a sense, a course in rational conduct. So far as moral precepts are concerned, one cannot find fault with the industry and earnestness of the heathen.[14]

In the same series of lectures, while dealing with the creation story, Luther makes the following observation about Aristotle's teachings on the heavenly bodies:

> These ideas, to be sure, are not certain; nevertheless, they are useful for teaching because they are the result of plausible reasoning and contain the foundation of the arts. Therefore it would be boorish to pay no attention to them or to regard them with contempt, especially since in some respects they are in agreement with experience.[15]

Not only does Luther have positive words
for reason and philosophy, but he also demonstrates
concern for and the use of reason in his own
theological works. One of the more interesting
examples of Luther's use of logic can be found
where he takes Erasmus to task for concluding that
a command necessarily implies the ability to fulfill
the command. Erasmus errs, says Luther, by inferring
an indicative meaning from an imperative verb.[16]
In his <u>Theses</u> <u>Concerning</u> <u>Faith</u> <u>and</u> <u>Law</u>, Luther pays
his respects to reason by structuring a syllogism
to make his point more clearly.[17] And for an
example of Luther calling reason to his aid in the
explication of a classical doctrine, one can cite
a passage from his exposition of John's Gospel
where the reformer elaborates on the doctrine of
the Trinity.[18]

The friends of Luther, to be sure, have not
failed to defend Luther against the various charges
of irrationalism. The above illustrations have been
presented to show that Luther's attitude toward
reason was not one of disdain only.[19] Our problem,
at this point, is to seek to understand the ration-
ale for this apparently inconsistent attitude toward
reason. Was Luther merely adept at talking out of
both sides of his mouth, or is there some interpretive key which will control the tensions? In
approaching this task Lohse's warning is relevant:
" . . . one must be careful not to develop a
complete system of Luther's conception of reason
and revelation. Luther never wrote a compendium of
his theology. It was always with particular problems
of his own time that he dealt."[20] On the other hand,
however, Luther was a far more "systematic" thinker
than many of his opponents have allowed. So while
there may be a lack of any specific treatise on the
subject of reason from Luther's own pen, yet, in
Gerrish's words:

> The essentials of Luther's attitude towards
> reason and philosophy are not difficult to
> piece together. . . . All that is required is
> a careful examination and organization of some

73

of the allusions . . . scattered throughout
his writings.[21]

From one point of view, Luther's stance
against reason and philosophy can be understood
historically. Sixteenth century Europe had moved
some distance from the speculative atmosphere of
high scholasticism; and the humanists of Europe,
who no doubt represented part of the "modern"
thrust of the culture, showed a certain disdain
for the scholastic method while their practical
bent was displayed in their preference for ethics
over theology as such.[22] Grimm's comment on
Erasmus reflects the setting: "The discussions of
such doctrines as the immaculate conception of
Mary, popular in the Sorbonne at the time, made him
contemptuous of the mental symnastics of traditional theology."[23] If Luther showed some weariness
toward scholasticism, he was not alone. Yet our
solution is not found, as such, in this historical
observation.

At this point it will be helpful to attempt
to grasp just what Luther meant by "reason."
Summarizing an older study by Hans Preuss, Robert
Fischer suggests that Luther uses the term ratio
in two general ways.[24] (1) Reason as meaning a
logical method. Luther used reason in this sense
without hesitation. It was an important element
in the many disputations held in the educational
enterprise of the university. Furthermore, in his
controversies with such men as Zwingli and Erasmus,
Luther not only seeks to be logical himself, but
he often berates his opponents for not being
sufficiently logical. (2) Reason "as the presupposition and the normative principle of all social
and cultural life. Here the term includes what
we would call 'common sense.'" This sense of
reason was also affirmed by Luther--as we can see
from the quotations above where he cites Aesop and
Cicero as able guides in good conduct and where he
suggests that man's reason is quite capable of helping him meet the various demands of everyday life.
Cranz sums up Luther's meaning of "reason" nicely
when he writes that reason is that "all-embracing
term which best refers to man's principle of action

74

in the realm of the world of civil justice, natural
law, and polity."[25]

In addition to these helpful comments from
Fischer on the meaning of "reason" for Luther, we
would suggest that where the reformer speaks most
disdainfully of reason he is using the word with
the connotation of "rationalization." For Luther
never seems impressed with the reasoning, as such,
of his opponents. As we have indicated, he
delights in picking their arguments apart--a feat
he accomplishes with some skill at times--to show
not only that the opponents position is unbiblical,
but that it also fails in logic or in proper understanding of grammar. The implication, then, is that
the so-called "reason" of his opponents--be they
fanatics, Zwinglians, or humanists--is really a
type of rationalization whereby they seek to justify
their misguided understanding of man's relationship
to God.[26]

The problem, it seems, may not be so much
in reason as such, but in the man who seeks to use
it. This brings us to a consideration of the state
and use of reason in fallen humanity as Luther understands it. For Luther, fallen man or natural man is
man as "flesh," to use Paul's term. By this term
Luther, as Paul, does not mean the physical lusts
of man as a physical being, but man as he is in his
totality, untouched and unredeemed by the Spirit of
God. This natural man is characterized by
concupiscentia--again, a term which, for Luther,
does not refer primarily to sexual lust, but to the
self-assertion and self-seeking which affects and
corrupts all aspects of man's activity.[27] Perhaps
the most apt phrase Luther used in describing man
in his fallen state is the one which describes man
as incurvatus in se, "turned in upon himself." In
this phrase we catch all the overtones of man as
sinner--man in his egocentricity, pride, idolatry,
rebellion and self-love. As one of man's most
important characteristics, reason is caught up in
and expresses this self-centeredness in its most
demonic forms.

Yet reason, itself, is not the dominant factor in man's activity, for reason is instrumental in its character. "It is always used for something or by something deeper than itself. With natural man reason is determined by self-will."[28] In his radical understanding of sin, Luther sees that sin is "mainly situated in the human will and consists in the self-will of man as opposed to God. . . ." The problem is not so much that man's capacity to reason is destroyed, but that reason, being directed by an ego-centric will, becomes distorted in its applications. "Reason is dominated by will . . . man sins with his will earlier than with his reason, though not chronologically, but logically. Or in other words, sin is something deeper than reason."[29] Thus the root of the problematic nature of reason lies in the fact that man tends to see only what he wants to see. It seems significant that Luther's exchange with Erasmus deals with the problem of man's will, and only secondarily with man's reason.[30] The root, then, of Luther's suspicions about reason lies in his anthropology. Reason is dominated by the will, and the will is incurvatus in se and is in bondage to this self. Later in this chapter we shall investigate the possibility of a "healed" reason in Luther's thought.

While reason is dominated by a will that is, in natural man, in bondage to self, yet it has its own proper place in the human economy. This proper place is in the area of political, domestic, and natural affairs. "The Kingdom of Reason embraces such human activities as caring for a family, building a home, serving as a magistrate, and . . . looking after cows."[31] In his large commentary on Galatians, Luther, in speaking of reason's place, asserts:

The natural endowments are indeed sound, but which natural endowments? Those by which a man who is drowned in wickedness and is a slave of the devil has a will, reason, free choice, and power to build a house, to carry on a governmental office, to steer a ship, and to do other

76

tasks that have been made subject to man.
. . .32

As our earlier quotation regarding Aesop and Cicero
indicated, Luther maintains that the moral conduct
of life is an area where reason might properly
operate. In our first chapter we saw that Luther
understood the natural law as an aspect of the
Divine Law. This natural law can, indeed must,
be delineated by reason since it is not the priv-
ileged task of the theologian as such.

> We must remember, . . . that Luther regards
> the details of the natural law, like the
> details of civil justice or of polity, as not
> within his proper competence as a theologian,
> and what he has to say about it is limited.
> He must as a theologian see that it remains
> within its proper realm, but it is finally up
> to reason and to philosophy to determine its
> content.33

Nor does Luther see ethics as the only
autonomous field of rational endeavor. Jaroslav
Pelikan argues persuasively that Luther had a
stance which allowed for the autonomy of each field
of science or reason. Pelikan writes:

> Despite his well-publicized remark about "that
> fool" Copernicus, who was trying to "turn all
> of astronomy upside down," Luther insisted
> that the study of the natural world, like the
> study of law or politics, had a technical
> autonomy and was to be permitted to carry out
> its research according to its own canons.34

This observation can be supported by citations from
Luther's lectures on the Genesis creation stories
where he writes:

> . . . I believe that this maxim is useful:
> Every science should make use of its own
> terminology, and one should not for this
> reason condemn the other or ridicule it; but
> one should rather be of use to the other, and

77

they should put their achievements at one
another's disposal. This is what craftsmen
do to maintain the whole city, which, as
Aristotle says, cannot be composed of a
physician and another physician but of a
physician and a farmer.
. . . .
But I am giving no consideration to these ideas
/his own ideas about astronomy/, for the
astronomers are the experts from whom it is
most convenient to get what may be discussed
about these subjects.[35]

Finally, as an example of the reformer's respect
for the scientific disciplines, a quote from his
lectures on Genesis:

Even though this science /astronomy/ has many
superstitious elements, still it should not be
completely disregarded; for as a whole it
concerns itself with the observation and
contemplation of the divine works, something
which is a most worthy concern in a human
being. Therefore men of the highest ability
have engaged in it and have taken delight in
it.[36]

Gerrish sums up Luther's understanding of reason's
proper domain nicely:

Reason is able to found kingdoms and common-
wealths, to fence them in and make them firm
with useful laws, to direct and govern them
with good counsel and sound precepts, to
prescribe many things indispensable for the
preservation of . . . human society. . . .
Reason, in fact, is the "soul of law and
mistress of all laws." The philosophy of
government rests upon the principle that reason
(in a sufficiently liberal amount) is the
possession of the few, whilst laws prescribed
by reason must serve for the many.[37]

From this angle of vision it seems clear

that there is nothing inherently obscurantist about
Luther's approach to reason, science, or philosophy.
As a matter of fact, it could be argued that Luther
helped to free both philosophy and science from the
presuppositions and structures of religious dogma--
an observation which will be clarified in the following paragraphs. No doubt the final word on Luther's
impact on philosophy in the West has yet to be
written. At this point we offer some quotations
from various scholars which indicate some difference
of opinion, to say the least. Bernhard Lohse writes,

> /Luther/ does not exclude all philosophical
> thinking as he is sometimes blamed for doing.
> Not only the fact that Luther praises human
> reason as God's highest gift to men, but also
> the fact that his definition of reason is not
> a static one leaves an open field for philosoply. [38]

The same general attitude, with a different twist,
is reflected in Heine's comment:

> . . . since Luther's time . . . men have
> disputed in the market-place, in the German
> popular tongue, without reserve or fear. The
> princes who accepted the Reformation legitimized
> this freedom of thought, of which one of the
> most important results is German philosophy. [39]

A dissenting note should be permitted. Maritain
labels Luther an "enemy of philosophy," and then
observes:

> Reason was very weak in him. If by intelligence
> we mean capacity to grasp the universal, to
> discern the essential, to follow humbly the
> wanderings and refinements of reality, then he
> was not intelligent, but shallow,--stubborn,
> especially. [40]

But if reason is to be limited to its "proper"
sphere, the implication is that reason is out of
bounds in other areas. Luther suggests this delineation:

79

In temporal affairs and those which have to do
with men, the rational man is self-sufficient.
. . . But in godly affairs, that is, in those
which have to do with God, where man must do
what is acceptable with God and be saved
thereby--here, however, nature is absolutely
stone-blind, so that it cannot even catch a
glimpse . . . of what those things are. It is
presumptuous enough to bluster and plunge into
them, like a blind horse; but all its conclusions
are utterly false, as surely as God lives.[41]

Reason is moving beyond its proper domain when it
seeks to deal with the ultimate issues of life,
when it seeks to trespass into the realm of redemption, when it pretends to elaborate on the ways and
means of man's salvation. Luther states the matter
strongly in his lectures on Galatians:

For the realm of human reason must be separated
as far as possible from the spiritual realm. . . .
I distinguish the natural endowments from the
spiritual; and I say that the spiritual endowments are not sound but corrupt, in fact totally
extinguished through sin in man and in the
devil. Thus there is nothing there but a
depraved intellect and a will that is hostile
and opposed to God's will--a will that thinks
nothing except what is against God. . . . In
divine matters, therefore, man has nothing but
darkness, error, malice, and perversity of will
and of intellect.[42]

In ultimate matters, then, reason is not only blind,
but it is perverse and corrupt, it seeks its own
way rather than God's way. Furthermore, natural
reason is offended by God's truth. In his strongly
worded reply to Erasmus, Luther writes:

So one of the main reasons why the words of
Moses and Paul are not taken in their plain
sense is their "absurdity". . . . And who is
offended by it? It is human reason that is
offended; which, though it is blind, deaf,
senseless, godless, and sacrilegious, in its

80

dealing with all God's words and works, is at
this point brought in as judge of God's word
and works! On these grounds you will deny all
the articles of the faith, for it is the highest absurdity by far . . . that God should be
man, a virgin's son, crucified, sitting at the
Father's right hand. It is, I repeat, <u>absurd</u>
to believe such things.[43]

Clearly Luther seeks to delineate the proper areas for reason's operations from the improper.
To explain why he makes this delineation, we must put
the problem within the broader scope of Luther's
thought.[44] While Luther's assertions about reason
and philosophy may appear to be inconsistent from
some perspectives, the reformer did not feel that he
was inconsistent from his own perspective.[45]

Let us first of all put Luther within the
historical setting that was his. It was an age that
reflected a strong sense of guilt and which pictured
Christ himself as a judge consigning some souls to
bliss and others to eternal damnation. As Roland
Bainton points out, the "best sellers" of the day
" . . . were not on <u>How to See Rome</u>, but on <u>How to
Avoid Hell</u>."[46] It was in this atmosphere that Luther
developed, and it was out of this setting that he
developed his deep soul-thirst for a gracious God.
It was to assure himself of God's gracious will toward him that Luther took the monastic vows so that
through the discipline, prayer, meditation and
asceticism of the monastic order he might somehow
attain that perfect love toward God and man which
God's commandments required of him.[47] It was,
indeed, <u>in</u> the monastic life, though not <u>through</u>
it as a means, that Luther found his gracious God.
Watson describes it well:

Deliverance came through the Gospel, not
because by it he was enabled to attain perfect
contrition and secure the grace that would
make him acceptable to God, but because it
revealed to him that God in His grace freely
forgave his inability to do so and
accepted him, unworthy as he was and in

81

spite of his sin. In other words, Luther gained a new conception of God—or rather, he entered into a new relationship to God, a relationship established not on the basis of Luther's righteousness—his fulfilment of the commandment of love toward God according to the Law—but on the basis of God's righteousness— God's fulfillment of His promises of love, according to the Gospel, toward Luther.[48]

It was this discovery of the gracious God in Christ through the Gospel (and which was the Gospel) that became the center of focus for Luther's theology. Whenever Luther seeks to sum up the chief message of the Christian faith, he does so in terms of such a central focus, although he may express this focus from different angles. Luther writes, "This is the true meaning of Christianity, that we are justified by faith in Christ, not by the works of the Law."[49] And some pages later, in his discussion of Galatians 2:16 ("yet who know that a man is not justified by works of the law but through faith in Jesus Christ . . ."), he asserts that Paul, in those words, had "summarized the chief doctrine of Christianity."[50] In a sermon at Weimar in 1522 he sounds the same theme: "Moreover, the gospel proclaims nothing else but salvation by grace, given to man without any works and merits whatsoever."[51] The influential Swedish scholar, Einar Billing, suggests the following as the primary focus in seeking to interpret Luther:

> Anyone wishing to study Luther would indeed be in no peril of going astray were he to follow this rule: never believe that you have a correct understanding of a thought of Luther before you have succeeded in reducing it to a simple corallary of the forgiveness of sins.[52]

What, then, has this to do with Luther's attitude toward reason and philosophy? Luther was convinced that natural man and his reason threatened the godliness of God in that reason always wants to invent some means for self-salvation. Reason

82

never manages to grasp the Gospel's truth--that forgiveness and salvation are God's free gift through Christ--but always thinks that man must somehow find a way to merit the grace of God. Thus, while Luther is more than happy to let reason have its field in the penultimate matters of family, home, nation, and vocation, he fences reason, as an originator or source, out of the field of theological endeavor.

Reason must be guarded from the theological sphere because it fails to recognize either the depth of or the solution to the human dilemma.

> In the first place, people are blind to their ailment; in the second place, they are ignorant of the remedy. Whoever considers himself hale and hearty is not interested in a physician; for first, he does not believe that he is ill, and, secondly, he knows of no physician or remedy for sickness. This is two-fold blindness. Here reason declines to see our wounds and sickness, and it also fails to yearn for healing and consolation.[53]

Reason is blind to the human ailment in that it does not discern that man stands totally condemned under the Law and that the Law is not a means by which man can justify himself before God. Reason argues that we must try to "work our way up from down here, assuming that the satisfaction resides within us." Reason has its own understanding of how one becomes reconciled with God. Luther has Reason say:

> If you have sinned, do penance and perform good works to redeem your sins. Become a monk or a nun; make God the triple vow of chastity, poverty, and obedience. In this way you will also have a supply of supererogatory works which you can transfer to others.[54]

In short, reason sees obedience to the Law as the means and method of salvation. The man unredeemed by grace finds it impossible to think

that the law is a weak and beggarly element,
useless for righteousness. In fact, he supposes
the very opposite about the Law, namely, not
only that it is necessary for salvation, but
that those who keep it merit righteousness and
eternal salvation.[55]

The source of this blindness is to be
found not only in the machinations of the devil, but
more surely in the distortions of the human will.
Speaking of the inborn knowledge of the Law of God,
Luther writes, "Nevertheless, human reason is so
corrupted and blinded by the malice of the devil
that it does not understand this inborn knowledge;
or, even if it has been admonished by the Word of
God, it deliberately neglects and despises it."[56]
On the other hand when carnal man discovers the
demand of the Law, his will is set over against the
demands and the Law itself.

Moses fled in horror when the rod he had cast
on the ground became a serpent. The same
thing happens when a man who is ignorant of
the law, and is therefore wont not to observe
it, is informed of the law, he becomes surly
and loaths the law, and he looks back with
sadness to the liberty from which he is now
cut off.[57]

Not only does fallen human nature tend to hate the
Law which makes such demands, but it also wishes
to cling to the claims of meritorious works.

Natural man cannot abide, hear, or see the
gospel. Nor does it enter into the hypocrites,
for it casts out their works, declaring that
they are nothing and not pleasing to God.
Therefore nature is constantly fighting against
the gospel; it will not tolerate it.[58]

In the light of this analysis it seems clear
that Luther's critique of reason is grounded not so
much in epistemology as it is in soteriology.
Luther is not primarily concerned about what is
"true," rather he is concerned about what is "saving."

Or, to put this in another way, Luther is concerned
about what is "saving" because, in the area of ultimate matters, of ultimate concern, only that which
is "saving" can be "true." Convinced that he understands man's dilemma—that man is guilty before God
and the Law and is in peril of death and condemnation
—Luther finds the solution not in man's works, but
in God's grace. Man's good works, be they intellectual or moral, are of no avail in spite of natural
man's reason which insists that man must and should
do at least something to acquire a right relationship with God. Instead, insists the reformer, man
must listen to the Gospel revealed through God's
Word.[59] Only there does man find that truth which
is redeeming, the truth that sets free. Only there
does man find himself forgiven and accepted.[60] In
one of his clearest statements of this concern for
saving faith and salvation by grace alone through
faith, the Reformer puts it this way:

> Here /regarding the doctrine of justification/
> let reason be far away, that enemy of faith,
> which, in the temptations of sin and death,
> relies not on the righteousness of faith or
> Christian righteousness, of which it is complete-
> ly ignorant, but on its own righteousness or,
> at most, on the righteousness of the Law. As
> soon as reason and the Law are joined, faith
> immediately loses its virginity. For nothing
> is more hostile to faith than the Law and
> reason; nor can these two enemies be overcome
> without great effort and work, and you must
> overcome them if you are to be saved.[61]

Gerrish sums our considerations up nicely as he
states the central thesis of his book:

> Luther's "irrationalism" is not to be inter-
> preted simply as a call for the theologian to
> abandon the demands of disciplined thought.
> Reason, as he understood it, constitutes a
> threat to the freedom of divine forgiveness,
> and his polemic is maintained chiefly in
> defence of the notion of God's "grace."[62]

85

We are now in position to show how Luther's
attitude toward reason can be set into the context
of his encounters with his opponents--both the
"fanatics," as he was wont to call the radical
fringe of the reformation, and the scholastic theologians. Luther's strongest blasts against reason
(the often quoted "devil's whore" label) comes when
Luther directs his fire against fanaticism
(Schwarmerei) in his last sermon in Wittenberg. Here
he complains that while the fanatics accept the Word
and faith, yet they "want to be wise in spiritual
things," and they "want to master both the Scriptures
and faith by their own wisdom."[63] While these
fanatics felt that St. Paul, the apostles and Luther
himself may have established a good beginning, they
seemed to be convinced, thought Luther, that they
were destined to bring the reformation and Christianity itself to its proper fulfillment.[64] Luther
considered this tendency to go beyond scripture not
only highly presumptuous but also as an open invita-
tion to heresy. This is the type of presumption which
the Devil incites when he is dressed up as an angel
of light.[65] It is interesting to note that Luther
sees the appeal to reason as one of the devil's most
potent weapons. Commenting that this "ancient
serpent" has in the past captured men's minds and
so deceived them he goes on to state:

> Nowadays he is showing his ability to do this
> in the fanatics, the Anabaptists, and the
> Sacramentarians. With his tricks he has so
> bewitched their minds that they are embracing
> lies, errors, and horrible darkness as the
> most certain truth and the clearest light.
> They will not permit themselves to be dissuaded
> from these dreams of theirs by admonitions of
> Scripture passages; for they are altogether
> persuaded that they alone are wise and have a
> pious attitude toward sacred things, and that
> everyone else is blind.[66]

A few sentences later Luther lists "Muntzer, Zwingli,
and others" as among those who have been bewitched.[67]

Building his case against the scholastics,

Luther accuses them of holding to a legalism which is rooted in the distortions of natural man's reason. In contrasting the nominalist position with that of St. Paul's, Luther exposes their distinctions between and uses of the "merits of congruity" and the "merits of condignity" as a perspective which diminishes or nullifies the need of Christ's death. Luther reasons:

> For if in a state of mortal sin I can do any tiny work that is not only pleasing before God externally and of itself but can even deserve grace "by congruity"; and if, once I have received grace, I am able to perform works according to grace, that is, according to love, and receive eternal life by a right--then what need do I have of the grace of God, the forgiveness of sins, the promise, and the death and victory of Christ?[68]

Although St. Thomas clearly differs from the nominalist position in that he understands all merits as gifts of God, yet Gerrish argues that Luther understood the Thomistic scheme still to be one of "legalism," for while <u>grace</u> is not earned, <u>salvation</u> is.[69] The break between Thomas and the reformer is clarified when we note that while, for Luther, justification and salvation are virtually synonymous, Thomas sees justification as the beginning of the road and not as salvation itself.[70] For Thomas, initial justification--which he identifies with the forgiveness of sins--starts man on the road to salvation in that it enables him to accomplish those good works, with the continual support of grace, of "faith formed by love" which ultimately free from sin. Grace makes merit possible, but merits are part of the redeeming process. Luther, himself, presses his argument in this form:

> For they /his opponents/ say that "infused faith," which they properly call faith in Christ, does not free from sin, but that only "faith formed by love" does so. From this it follows that faith in Christ by itself, without the Law and works, does not save. Surely this is to declare

87

that Christ leaves us in our sins and in the
wrath of God and makes us worthy of eternal
death. On the other hand, if you perform the
Law and works, then faith justifies, because it
has works, without which faith is useless.
Therefore, works justify, not faith. That because of which something is what it is, is itself more so. For if faith justifies because
of works, then works justify more than faith.[71]

While there may be some question about the adequacy
of Luther's understanding of Aquinas, the reformer
himself was convinced that the Thomistic solution in
general included a positive role of works and "merit,"
the latter of which Thomas defines as "the price paid
for work done."[72] In contrast, Luther sees no place
at all for "merits" in the message of salvation.

With Paul, therefore, we totally deny the "merit
of congruity" and the "merit of condignity";
and with complete confidence we declare that
these speculations are merely the tricks of Satan,
which have never been performed or demonstrated
by any examples. For God has never given anyone grace and eternal life for the merit of
congruity or the merit of condignity.[73]

In these statements we see how Luther links
the distorted presentation of the Christian message,
as he sees it, to the "speculations" of human reason
and the "tricks of Satan." Such, then, is the setting
for Luther's disdainful attitude toward Aristotle,
especially, and philosophy in general--as it seeks to
intrude into theology.[74] Luther's diatribes against
that "pagan philosopher" Aristotle and against
scholastic theology are grounded in the attempted
synthesis of philosophy and theology which results
in a synthesis of grace and works, thereby nullifying
the totally unmerited aspect of God's grace in Christ.
Thomas becomes the special object of the Reformer's
wrath since Luther saw him as the culprit who brought
Aristotle into the schools.[75]

At this point a reminder and a question must

be expressed. The reminder: In spite of Luther's insistence that reason must be fenced out of theology, yet the Reformer obviously uses reason a great deal in his own theologizing. We recall our earlier statements about the positive side and the positive role of reason in Luther's thinking and theory. The question, then, is this: How does Luther justify his own obvious use of reasoning when he speaks theologically? To put the question in another form, we ask: Is there another type of reason, a "healed" reason, which a Christian theologian uses--some kind of epistemological vantage point by which the theologian discerns the scene? It seems that Luther's solution to this epistemological question is the same as his solution to the soteriological question. The question is answered by "faith"--one might say sola fide. For Luther does submit that there is a "right reason" which comes to play from out of the stance of faith.

Luther works out this point of view in a lengthy section of his lectures on Galatians where he elaborates on verse 3:10, "For all who rely on works of the law are under a curse; for it is written, 'cursed be every one who does not abide by all things written in the book of the law, and do them.'" The solution to the epistemological problem comes, interestingly, within the context of the solution to the moral and soteriological problems. Luther argues that since a good tree must precede good fruit (Matthew 7:17), and, in moral philosophy, a good will must precede a good act, so, in theological "doing" there must be a precondition. This precondition is faith. "In theology, therefore, 'doing' necessarily requires faith itself as a precondition."[76] Thus when a theologian seeks to interpret those passages of Scripture which refer to "works" and "doing," as Romans 2:13 and II Peter 1:10, he must understand these as "theological terms," not "moral or natural ones." That is to say, such works and doings must always be linked to and grow out of faith, which is prior. "When we theologians speak about 'doing,' therefore, it is necessary that we speak about doing with faith, because in

89

theology we have no right reason and good will except faith."[77]

> The governing principle of conduct in the believer is no longer natural reason, but reason enlightened by faith. Faith virtually takes the place of reason; right reason in spiritual matters is faith. . . . Reason is still reason, even in the domain of theology, but now it is illuminated by faith: it is "right reason" in a theological sense.[78]

Since "right reason" is grounded in faith, Luther is not suspicious of the cognitive aspect of faith. Faith is not empty of content. There are certain assertions that are part of the faith stance; Christian faith is not faith in faith. In speaking about the doctrines involved in the birth, suffering, death, and resurrection of the God-Man Luther writes:

> We must look at this image and take hold of it with a firm faith. He who does this has the innocence and the victory of Christ, no matter how great a sinner he is. But this cannot be grasped by loving will; it can be grasped only by reason illumined by faith. Therefore we are justified by faith alone, because faith alone grasps this victory of Christ.[79]

One needs only to remember Luther's heated response to Erasmus when the latter suggested that he found little satisfaction in assertions and would gladly have taken up the Sceptic's position insofar as Scripture and Church would permit.

> What Christian can endure the idea that we should deprecate assertions? That would be denying all religion and piety in one breath--asserting that religion and piety and all dogmas are just nothing at all. Why then do you--you!--assert that you find no satisfaction in assertions and that you prefer an undogmatic temper to any other.[80]

For Luther there are assertions to be made about the saving aspect of the Christ event. These are assertions made out of "right reason," a reason healed and enlightened by faith. The Christian asserts that Christ is his redemption, sanctification, righteousness, and "wisdom."[81] This is a reason which expresses the entire man made whole. It is an involved, an existential reason, not an abstract or merely academic reason. It is a reason grounded in God's Word, and is, therefore, a reason which understands savingly.

> Faith is nothing else but the truth of the heart, that is, the right knowledge of the heart about God. But reason cannot think correctly about God; only faith can do so. A man thinks correctly about God when he believes God's Word. But when he wants to measure and to believe God apart from the Word, with his own reason, he does not have the truth about God in his heart and therefore cannot think or judge correctly about Him.[82]

Having outlined Luther's attitude toward reason and philosophy and their proper role in the various spheres of existence, let us now turn our attention to the role of reason in the understanding of God and His relationship to the world and to mankind. In the first place, it seems clear that Luther held to some kind of "natural knowledge" of God. In a number of contexts Luther asserts that the reality of God is apparent to man as man, without any special role of "revelation."[83] Commenting on Romans 1:19-20, Luther states:

> This means that, from the creation of the world, it has always been the case that the "invisible things of him are clearly seen," and this is said in order that nobody may cavil and say that only in our time it was possible to know God. For it has been possible to know him from the beginning of the world and at all times, and it is possible now. . . . That . . . the knowledge of God was open to all men, and especially to idolaters, so that they are without excuses

91

when it is proved to them that they had known
the invisible things of God, namely, his very
divinity and eternity and power, can plainly
be demonstrated by the fact that all who made
idols for themselves worshiped them and called
them gods or God, believing that God was
immortal (i.e., eternal) and also capable and
able to help, thereby giving clear evidence that
they had the knowledge of God in their hearts.
For how could they call a picture or some other
created thing God, or believe that created things
resembled him, if they had no knowledge of God
and what pertains to him?[84]

Almost two decades later, Luther has this section
of Romans in mind while lecturing on Galatians:

By nature all men have the general knowledge
that there is a God, according to the statement
on Romans 1:19-20: . . . Besides, the forms of
worship and the religions that have been and
remained among all nations are abundant evidence
that at some time all men have had a general
knowledge of God. . . . All men have the general
knowledge, namely, that God is, that He has
created heaven and earth, that He is just, that
He punishes the wicked, etc.[85]

From another perspective, Luther offers what
might be designated as a type of "moral sense" of
the reality of God:

Reason is familiar with the knowledge of God
which is based on the Law. It almost got hold
of and sniffed God, for from the Law it saw
the difference between right and wrong. The
Law is also inscribed in our hearts. . . . All
rational beings can of themselves determine
that it is wrong to disobey father and mother
. . . steal, curse, and blaspheme. . . . They
have the content of the Law of God and the Ten
Commandments written in their hearts by nature.[86]

Less often, Luther moves into a variation

on the cosmological argument, as in the context
of his lectures on the creation narrative. After
observing that the heavens, since they are "watery,"
require a stability introduced from an exterior
power, Luther comments:

> The more observant among the philosophers drew
> from this source what is in truth not an
> insignificant proof: that all things are done
> and guided, not planlessly but by divine
> providence, inasmuch as the movements of the
> masses on high and of heaven are so definite
> and unique. Who would say that they are
> accidental or purely a matter of nature when
> the objects fashioned by artisans--such as
> round or three-cornered or six-cornered columns--
> are not accidental but the result of definite
> plan and skill.[87]

The reformer's acceptance of such a natural
knowledge of God is no doubt rooted in the Scriptures
themselves, as Luther understands them, for he often
quotes Romans 1:19-20 as the biblical basis for this
assertion. Yet, as we have seen, Luther moves beyond
this scriptural source--or, we might say, he extra-
polates from this source--and suggests other reasons
for accepting such a knowledge. In summary, the
reasons he suggests include: 1) a "linguistic
argument" wherein he suggests that even an idolater
must have some meaningful concept of what the word
"God" means since he applies such a term to his
idols; 2) the more common "argument from universality," which concludes the existence of such a
natural knowledge of God from the fact that all
nations and peoples express some type of worship
and religion; 3) the "moral argument" wherein man's
natural knowledge of God is reflected in his knowledge of moral demands made upon him; and 4) the
"cosmological argument" or "argument from design"--
assuming the authenticity of such passages.

But Luther will not let us rest with any
simple view, for he often reflects a position which
seems diametrically opposed to the one elaborated
above. In one context Luther seems to deny outright

any knowledge of God outside of revealed knowledge:

> God does not want to be known except through
> Christ; nor, according to John 1:18, can He be
> known in any other way. . . . Therefore Christ
> alone is the means, the life, and the mirror
> through which we see God and know His will.[88]

In another setting, while Luther extols the various
virtues of the heathen, he states this about their
knowledge of God:

> Yet we maintain that /their/ loftiest thoughts
> about God, about the worship of God, and about
> the will of God are a darkness more than
> Cimmerian. The light of reason, which has
> been granted to man alone, has insight only
> into what benefits the body.[89]

In much the same mood the Reformer gives warning
against any attempt to know God aside from His
revelation:

> You have often heard from us that it is a
> rule and a principle . . . to refrain from
> speculation about the majesty of God, which is
> too much for the human body, and especially
> for the human mind, to bear. . . Nothing is
> more dangerous than to stray into heaven with
> our idle speculations, there to investigate
> God in His incomprehensible power, wisdom,
> and majesty. . . .[90]

A citation, which we have quoted earlier in this
chapter, not only involves a negative attitude about
the natural knowledge of God, but also provides the
possibility of an interprative key for the apparent
inconsistency in Luther's thinking in this area:

> But reason cannot think correctly about God;
> only faith can do so. A man thinks correctly
> about God when he believes God's Word. But
> when he wants to measure and to believe God
> apart from the Word, with his own reason, he
> does not have the truth about God in his heart,
> and therefore cannot think or judge correctly
> about Him.[91]

How is this tension to be reconciled? On the one hand "By nature all men have the general knowledge that there is a God," yet, on the other hand, "Christ alone is the means, the life, and the mirror through which we see God. . . ." This tension is to be resolved in the same way that Luther resolves the tension between his attack on reason and his praise of reason. Here, again, our interpretation must be controlled by a fundamental soteriological focus. Just as there is a role for reason outside the realm of salvation, even so there is a natural knowledge of God; but such knowledge is never, for Luther, a saving knowledge. In what is, perhaps, the clearest expression of Luther's solution to this tension, he writes:

There is a twofold knowledge of God: The general and the particular. All men have the general knowledge, namely, that God is, that He has created heaven and earth, that He is just, that He punishes the wicked, etc. But what God thinks of us, what He wants to give and to do to deliver us from sin and death and to save us -- which is the particular and the true knowledge of God--this men do not know. Thus it can happen that someone's face may be familiar to me but I do not really know him, because I do not know what he has in his mind. So it is that men know naturally that there is a God, but they do not know what He wants and what He does not want.[92]

More quotations should be considered which will restate this "twofold" knowledge, but which will express the "general" and the "particular" types of knowledge in other terms thus bringing in the methodological implications more clearly. First, refering to the "moral" knowledge of God, Luther writes:

There are two kinds of knowledge of God: The one is the knowledge of the Law; the other is the knowledge of the Gospel. For God issued the Law and the Gospel that he might be known through them. Reason is familiar with the knowledge of God which is based on the Law. . . . But the

95

knowledge of God derived from the Law is not the
true knowledge of Him, . . .[93]

Elsewhere, Luther contrasts the "evangelical" or
saving knowledge of God, with the "partial" knowledge of reason:

> . . . the true and thorough knowledge and way of
> thinking about God . . . is called the knowledge
> of grace and truth, the "evangelical knowledge
> of God. But this knowledge does not grow up in
> our garden, and nature knows nothing at all about
> it. Reason has only a left-handed and a partial
> knowledge of God, based on the law of nature and
> of Moses. . . . /But/ that all men are born in
> sin and are damned, that Christ, the Son of God,
> is the only source of grace, and that man is
> saved solely through Jesus Christ, who is grace
> and truth--that is not Mosaic or legal knowledge,
> but evangelical and Christian knowledge.[94]

This last citation not only elaborates on the nature
of the twofold knowledge of God, but it also suggests
the source and ground for the genuine or "evangelical"
knowledge of God--the revelation in Christ. Here,
indeed, is Christocentric theology. For while man
does have some general knowledge about God, such as
His eternal nature, and His demands through the Law,
yet significant knowledge in the sense of saving
knowledge comes only through the Gospel of Christ.
In Christ only does man discover God's <u>attitude</u> and
<u>will</u> toward him; here only does man find himself
forgiven, though a sinner; here only is guilt overcome and death defeated; here only is the gracious
God discovered.

But the natural knowledge of God is not only
inadequate in terms of redemption, it also stands
as the source of all forms of idolatry. "From the
acceptance of this major premise, 'There is a God,'
there came all the idolatry of men, which would
have been unknown in the world without the knowledge
of the Diety."[95] Thus, in Luther's mind, man has
the option of various kinds of idolatry, or the
possibility of valid worship of God through Christ.

96

Man's _general_ knowledge of God tempts him to develop
a _particular_ knowledge. In this way man's reason and
imagination produce images of God contrary to His
real nature. "Thus a monk imagines a God who forgives
sins and grants grace and eternal life because of the
observance of his rule." This kind of God, Luther
insists, has never existed. The monk's image of God
is an idol; a God who justifies man only on the basis
of man's works, be they works of obedience to the
Monastic vows or of obedience to the Law, is sheer
fiction and no God at all. At this point we find
that we have returned to the central theme of Luther's
theological reflection--justification by grace alone
through faith alone. Luther ties the proper knowledge of God to justification in the following manner:

> Whoever falls from the doctrine of justification
> is ignorant of God and is an idolater. There-
> fore it is all the same whether he then returns
> to the Law or to the worship of idols; it is all
> the same whether he is called a monk or a Turk
> or a Jew or an Anabaptist. For once this doctrine
> is undermined, nothing more remains but sheer
> error, hypocrisy, wickedness, and idolatry, . . .
> The reason is this: God does not want to be known
> except through Christ; . . .
> . . . .
> Apart from Christ there is nothing but sheer
> idolatry, an idol and a false fiction about
> God, . . .[96]

To cast this discussion briefly in another form, one
can observe that, for Luther, whatever might be the
channels by which man becomes aware of his
predicament, the saving answer comes only by God's
grace through revelation. The Gospel as the answer
to man's deepest need is not ascertained through human
reason, but becomes livingly and knowingly real to
man only through God's saving work accomplished
through Christ, witnessed to by the Scriptures, and
imparted to man's heart through the Holy Spirit who
awakens man to faith.[97]

Luther would, of course, insist that a
saving or "evangelical" knowledge of God is not to

be understood in any purely formal way, as if such
knowledge were a matter of obtaining a clearer
philosophic or doctrinal statement of what God is
like.[98] To know God revealed through Christ is not
to receive new information about God, but to find
oneself living in a new relationship with the
Divine. Such knowledge does not so much inform, as
it transforms. The whole man is involved--mind,
emotion, will. The Christian man is not the man with
all the right theories, but the man in right relation--
a relation which makes him a "free lord of all,
subject to all."[99] Right knowledge, then, is an
existential knowing which transforms human attitudes
and existence:

> Behold, from faith thus flow forth love and joy
> in the Lord, and from love a joyful, willing
> and free mind that serves one's neighbor will-
> ingly and takes no account of gratitude or
> ingratitude, of praise or blame, of gain or
> loss.[100]

Surely Lohse is correct when he writes of Luther's
view: "If a man thinks that he knows something about
God and if this knowledge of his does not affect his
whole life . . . he really knows nothing about God."[101]
Or as Whale states it:

> A God whom we could discuss in a leisurely way,
> with our feet up, would not be the living God
> with whom we have to do, but an idol fashioned
> out of our aesthetic speculation. This is in
> part what Luther meant when he said: "To believe
> in God is to go down on your knees."[102]

    No consideration of Luther's understanding
of man's knowledge of God would be complete without
a presentation of his distinction between the
"hidden" and the "revealed" God, and his insistence
upon a "theology of the cross" as opposed to a
"theology of glory."[103] In both of these distinctions
Luther is making much the same point; God in His
essence, as He is in Himself, is not only beyond the
ken of human reason but also is not a proper object

for reason to pursue or seek to grasp. On the other hand, the "true" or evangelical knowledge of God which is revealed to man through the Word is not a knowledge of God in His essence, but a "relational" knowledge--a knowledge which speaks healingly to the human situation through various natural forms in which God "clothes" Himself. Here, again, Luther's stance is soteriologically determined. To know God aright--and let us remember that this "knowing" involves the total man--is to find oneself saved, anything short of this is neither significant nor "knowledge" in its proper theological sense.

Luther speaks of a "hidden" God because he believes that God in His essence is incomprehensible to fallen man. "No one can fathom Him, or climb to His heights. He is too lofty."[104] Since fallen man cannot see the "naked God"--God in His divine essence--and still live, God "covers" Himself and comes to man so that man might approach Him.[105] Luther suggests that Adam, before the Fall, might have been able to confront God without such a mediating cover; but the Fall has changed the situation.

> This nature of ours has become so misshapen through sin, so depraved and utterly corrupted, that it cannot recognize God or comprehend His nature without a covering. It is for this reason that those coverings are necessary.[106]

Not only is God in Himself beyond the categories of human reason, but it is also highly dangerous for man to seek to pry into the Glory of the transcendent God:

> . . . nothing is more dangerous than to stray into heaven with our idle speculations, there to investigate God in His incomprehensible power, wisdom, and majesty. . . . For as in His own nature God is immense, incomprehensible and infinite, so to man's nature He is intolerable.[107]

The danger lies not so much in the possibility of offending the Divine by such prying, but in the

99

threat to man's own salvation which arises out of such speculations. "Therefore," Luther continues, "if you want to be safe and out of danger to your conscience and your salvation, put a check on this speculative spirit." But what, in this speculation, constitutes the danger? Gerrish sums up the matter:

> To pry into the majesty of God is (at least in part) to endeavor to comprehend His will toward us by the judgment of reason, that is, without having recourse to God's Word. . . . And yet the real danger of the sensus speculationis lies . . . in its inability to calm the troubled conscience. To seek God elsewhere than in Christ is to find a God whose glory is not His grace, a God who can only be approached in the terror of a burdened conscience. . . . For the anxious sinner, not knowing God as He really is in Christ, resorts frantically to good works of his own invention in the forlorn effort to make God propitious. What may begin with the arrogance of superior wisdom and virtue may end with the torments of the afflicted conscience.[108]

But if God as He is in Himself is hidden from us, God as He would have us know Him is revealed to us savingly through various signs and images.

> Let it be the concern of each of us to abide by the signs which God has revealed . . . to us, namely, His Son, born of the Virgin Mary and lying in His manger among the cattle; the Word; Baptism; the Lord's Supper; and absolution. In these images we see and meet a God whom we can bear, one who comforts us, lifts us up into hope, and saves us.[109]

And of course all of these images and signs find their origin in Christ.

> The incarnate Son of Man is, therefore, the covering in which the Divine majesty presents Himself to us with all His gifts, and does so

in such a manner that there is no sinner too
wretched to be able to approach Him with the
full assurance of obtaining pardon. . . . We
must come to the Father by that way which is
Christ Himself; He will lead us safely, and
we shall not be deceived.[110]

     Luther's insistence upon a "theology of the
cross" rather than a "theology of glory" is directly
related to the distinction between the "hidden" and
the "revealed" God. Briefly, a theology of glory
is one which seeks to grasp the nature of God as He
is in Himself, God in His divine Glory, while a
theology of the cross is a "true" theology which
seeks to speak of God only on the basis of God's
condescending act in Jesus Christ. The true
theologian finds God revealed in the lowliness of
the Christ event.

Therefore begin where Christ began--in the
Virgin's womb, in the manger, and at His mother's
breasts. For this purpose He came down, was
born, lived among men, suffered, was crucified,
and died, so that in every possible way He
might present Himself to our sight. He wanted
to fix the gaze of our hearts upon Himself and
thus to prevent us from clambering into heaven
and speculating about the Divine majesty.[111]

     In his Heidelberg Disputation of 1518 Luther
characterizes the "theologians of glory" as those
who seek to interpret the invisible things of God "on
the basis of the things which have been created."
While on the other hand a theologian worthy of the
name is he who understands the "visible and hinder
parts of God to mean the passion and the cross."[112]
The concern, again, is for redemptive knowledge.
Such knowledge of God as man might obtain by inferring
from created things "does not make a man worthy or
wise." Rather, in Christ crucified is the true
theology and the knowledge of God." True theology
deals, always, with God for me as I find Him acting
in Christ. What God might be in Himself may be
interesting speculation, but such speculation has
no particular relationship to my broken human nature.

101

At this point we must consider more care-
fully what roles reason and revelation play in
man's understanding of the Law. More particularly
we will need to ask if some work of revelation or
some act of the Holy Spirit must transpire before
the "theological" use of the Law takes place. As
indicated in Chapter I, there seems to be little
doubt that Luther affirmed some "natural knowledge"
of the Law of God. That is to say, man as man has
some understanding of the moral structures of the
created universe which can be referred to as
"natural" Law. This natural Law is the Law of God.
The Law of Moses, as centered in the Ten Commandments, is not a new Law system, but it is a clarification of the natural Law which is "written on
man's heart." (However, God did give some special
ceremonial laws to the Jews which are not binding
on other nations.) Furthermore, natural man can
clearly understand by way of his own reason that
the whole of the Law can be summed up in the
command to love the neighbour as oneself. Regarding the "civil" use of the Law, we noted Luther's
assertion that man's reason here functions
appropriately and adequately. In the realm of
family, community, and nation, man must govern and
order by application of reason and common sense.

On the other hand, however, Luther does not
clearly conclude that the theological use of the
Law can be totally fulfilled through the use of
natural man's reason alone. Does the natural knowledge of the Law crush man's presumption, bring
him to despair of himself and thus drive him to
Christ? In the following passage, while Luther
elaborates on the matter of the natural Law being
written in man's heart, he seems to imply that the
Law does have the power, somehow, to bring man to
despair simply through confronting man with its
demands.

If the natural law were not written and given
in the heart by God, one would have to preach
long before the conscience were smitten. One
would have to preach to an ass, horse, ox, or
cow for a hundred thousand years before they

accepted the Law, . . . What is wrong? Their
soul is not so formed and fashioned that such
a thing might enter it. But a man, when the
Law is set before him, soon says: Yes, it is so,
he cannot deny it. He could not be so quickly
convinced, were it not written in his heart
before.[113]

In his lectures on Romans Luther reflects
the view that the natural knowledge of the Law
brings remorse to man's conscience. While arguing
that the Law is written in man's heart, he asserts
that man's feelings of remorse about his deeds
indicate that he does have a natural knowledge of
the Law. This remorse does not stem from the
attitudes of others or the opinions of others, it
stems from the witness of one's own conscience from
which one cannot flee.

So also God will judge all men according to
their inner thoughts, and he will disclose our
most secret thoughts of ourselves in such a
way that there will be no deeper inwardness or
secrecy to flee to. But our thoughts will lie
naked and open before all as if God were to say:
Behold, I do not judge you but assent to your
own judgment about yourself and confirm it,
and as you cannot judge differently about yourself, neither can I. According to the witness
of your thoughts and of your conscience, you
therefore, deserve either heaven or hell.[114]

Pinomaa seems to imply that the natural understanding of the Law can, in fact, perform the theological
function of the Law. "Luther sees the possibilities
of natural man in terms of this either-or: either
he is aware of the law, and being ignorant of God's
grace, falls into despair, or he is unaware of the
law and becomes proud, despising God's wrath."[115]
Seeberg reflects the same position when he writes of
Luther's theology:

Since the law thus presses upon man and he cannot inwardly and actually meet its demands,
there seizes him on the one hand, a terror at
the thought of God and desire to escape from

him; . . . But, on the other hand, a great
longing fills his heart to be free from this
pressure. This impels him toward Christ and
the gospel.[116]

One of the most striking statements on this issue
from Luther's own writings reads:

Thus we, too, when we are without grace and
in the Law, do the works of the Law like
slaves, . . . Nevertheless, we are instructed
by all this in such a way that we sigh for the
inheritance, that is for faith and grace, by
which we, snatched out of this state of
slavery, may fulfill the Law in the freedom
of the Spirit.[117]

While in his large commentary on Galatians he writes:

Therefore the Law cannot do anything except
that with its light it illumines the conscience
for sin, death, judgment, and the hate and
wrath of God. Before the Law comes, I am smug
and do not worry about sin; when the Law comes,
it shows me sin, death, and hell. Surely this
is . . . being sentenced, being made an enemy
of God, being condemned to death and hell.[118]

These various passages could be interpreted
to mean that Luther believed the theological
function of the Law, that of driving to despair and
in search of grace, might be accomplished through
natural man's encounter with the natural knowledge
of the Law alone, without a specific act of grace
or of the Holy Spirit. Yet such a view is never
explicitly stated. Furthermore, there are other
elements in Luther's thought that tend to suggest
the necessity of an alternative interpretation--
elements which indicate that natural knowledge of
the Law is not, in itself, an adequate preparation
for grace. God Himself must reveal man's true
plight to man. Gordon Rupp moves toward this view
as he analyzes Luther's understanding of the "whole
man" who stands either under sin or under grace.
"Luther's is an anthropology 'coram Deo.' This

truth about man is revealed by God, and only partly realized by man himself."[119]

Such an interpretation becomes feasible in the light of Luther's grave misgivings about reason's ability to grasp the depth of the human predicament. These reservations are reflected when Luther writes concerning the Law of love:

> They have it written in their hearts, of course, because by nature they judge that one should do to others what one wants done to oneself (Matt. 7:12). But it does not follow that they understand this. . . . The blindness of human reason is so incomprehensible and infinite that it cannot form sound judgments even about life and works, much less about doctrines of faith."[120]

In his unredeemed state man's reason seems meagre, at best. Human reason, while not destroyed, is so corrupted and blinded by the devil that it fails to understand the inborn knowledge of God. Even when admonished by the Word of God, reason tends to neglect and despise the Law.[121] In a sermon Luther states:

> In the first place, people are blind to their ailment; in the second place, they are ignorant of the remedy. Whoever considers himself hale and hearty is not interested in a physician; for first, he does not believe that he is ill, . . . Here reason declines to see our wounds and sickness, and it also fails to yearn for healing and consolation.[122]

If reason, then, is blind to the depth of man's predicament, man must come to a knowledge of his sickness through some other means. Rupp gives an interpretive direction: "It is revelation and not man's own insight, wisdom, or religious experience, which shows man his real predicament, and which reveals him to be 'coram deo' a sinner, unrighteous in all his acts, under condemnation."[123]

105

Rupp's interpretation can be supported by a number of references from Luther's writings. Before the Reformation battles began, Luther can assert: "For . . . by faith alone we must believe that we are sinners, for this is not obvious to us; indeed, quite often we are not even conscious of it."[124] While in one of the creative early years of the reforming movement Luther can say, "Therefore, the moment you begin to have faith, you learn that all things in you are altogether blameworthy, sinful, and damnable. . . ."[125]

In our first chapter we noted that the condemning aspect of the Law is prior to the knowledge and experience of grace in Luther's theological perspective, yet we find that the Gospel itself tends to clarify the demands of the Law and to press home the theological function of the Law.

> For without the knowledge of grace, that is, of the Gospel of Christ, it is impossible for a man to think that the Law is a weak and beggarly element, useless for righteousness. In fact, he supposes the very opposite about the Law, namely, not only that it is necessary for salvation, but that those who keep it merit righteousness and eternal salvation.[126]

This clarifying function of the Gospel is posited by Seeberg as he writes, "If it is therefore the chief office of the Gospel to proclaim grace and consolation, it yet deepens also the understanding of the law and humiliates and chastens the sinner."[127] Commenting on Luther's Law-Gospel structure in his critical chapter on Tillich, Robert Johnson makes the same point:

> . . . we must conclude that man can neither know the correct existential questions, nor find the intended Christian answers, except as he stands under the Word. . . . This crucial methodological assumption, that man can recognize his real plight and his true need only coram Deo, was intrinsic to the Reforma-

tion.[128]

This clarifying function of the Gospel can be cast in other terms--that of the work of the Holy Spirit. Since man is not able, through his own understanding, to recognize his plight, the Holy Spirit functions in a noetic role and man is awakened to his dilemma. In lecturing on John 16:8 ("And when He comes, He will convince the world of sin and of righteousness and of judgment."), Luther asserts:

> Well, here you hear Christ say that the Holy Spirit will "convince the world of sin," and that He will do this through the agency of these messengers of His. Therefore it is not they who do so; it is the Holy Spirit, at whose order and in whose office they are preaching.[129]

In the same vein, the Reformer writes in his Theses on Faith and Law: "36) Its force /the Law's/ . . . and power is to slay, or to show that sin must be punished with eternal death. 37) When a man really begins to feel this force, with the Spirit reproving him, he soon despairs of God's mercy."[130] While Köstlin quotes Luther as saying, "And it is false (to say) that the Law convinces of sin without the Holy Spirit, since the Law was written by the finger of God."[131] In the light of such accents, which can be abundantly cited in Luther's writings, Prenter's declaration seems clearly valid: the answer to the problem of man's knowledge of sin is to be found in the act of the Holy Spirit.[132]

We conclude, then, that while man's natural reason has some sense of the judging Law of God standing over against him, yet the full theological use of the Law with its impact of despair and utter self-abandonment does not take place without God's own presence as expressed through the Holy Spirit. In short, the right questions are never known without revelation. At the same time the Law-Gospel order is maintained. Knowledge of the Law in its theological thrust is still a necessary preliminary

107

to the good news of God's act in Christ. Thus the
Law must still be preached, for such preaching has
the function, through the work of the Holy Spirit,
to drive men to the Gospel. The preaching of the
Gospel alone is not adequate preparation for the
grace of Christ.[133] Man's natural understanding of
such Law may produce fear of God and the imperfect
penitence (attritio) of "Cain's repentence." While
this type of penitence may bear no spiritual fruit
in itself, it does provide a point of contact whereby the Holy Spirit may obtain a "foot-hold" into
the life of man.[134] Ultimately, it is God Himself who wounds in order to save.

FOOTNOTES

1. Walter Kaufmann, _Critique of Religion and Philosophy_ (Anchor Books; Garden City: Doubleday and Co., 1961), pp. 305 ff.

2. Arnold Lunn, _The Revolt Against Reason_ (London: Eyre and Spottiswoode, 1950), pp. 51 ff. Lunn displays a nice touch of English propriety when he chides Luther for being "oversexed" and for using foul language.

3. Jacques Maritain, _Three Reformers_ (New York: Charles Scribner's Sons, 1929), p. 34. In fine polemical style Maritain marshalls a number of quotations from Luther which reflect a disdainful attitude toward reason; but Maritain fails to make any attempt to put this attitude into the context of Luther's theological stance.

4. S.T., I, 155.

5. For some summaries of the various types of charges made against Luther on this point see: B. A. Gerrish, _op. cit._, pp. 1-3; R. H. Fischer, "A Reasonable Luther," _Reformation Studies_, ed. Franklin Littell (Richmond: John Knox Press, 1962), pp. 30 ff.; and Bernhard Lohse, _Ratio und Fides_ (Gottingen: Vandenhoeck & Ruprecht, 1958), pp. 7 ff.

6. A.E., LI, 374, (1546).

7. L.C.C., XV, 218, (1515-1516).

8. Ibid., p. 218.

9. Ibid., p. 236.

10. Gerrish, _op. cit._, p. 29. Gerrish cites W.A.TR. 5, No. 5245.

11. Ibid., p. 4.

12. A.E., XXXIV, 137, (1517); from _Disputation Concerning Man_.

13. W.A., X/I/I, 527; as translated and quoted by Gerrish, _op. cit._, p. 12.

14. A.E., II, 159-160, (ca. 1537). This is, to be sure, qualified praise.

15. A.E., I, 27, (1535).

16. Luther, _Bondage_ . . . , pp. 151 ff., (1525).

17. A.E., XXXIV, 118, (1535).

18. "For it stands to reason that there must be a listener where a speaker and a word are found." (A.E., XXIV, 364). Needless to say, Luther did _not_

consider the doctrine of the Trinity to be a
product of natural reason, nor even necessarily a
doctrine which natural reason can fathom.

   19. For a helpful view of "A Reasonable
Luther," see the article by that title by Robert H.
Fischer, op. cit. Fischer investigates Luther's use
of reason in several instances: 1) his appeal to
Scripture and reason in his stand at the Diet of
Worms, 1521; 2) his alleged contempt for mathematics
in the famous "two and five are eight"--if God so
tells me--passage; 3) his use of reason in his
battle with Erasmus over the bondage or freedom of
the will; 4) his battle with Zwingli over the meaning
of the Lord's Supper. In this last instance Luther
chides the Swiss for not using reason enough; and he
charges Zwingli with ignorance of grammar. Fischer
concludes: "The adequacy and permanence of Luther's
theology, of course, remain subject to dispute, but
one must acknowledge a massive consistency and
clarity and even power in his use of reason."

        For some excellent studies of the place of
reason in Luther's theology see: Gerrish, op. cit;
Lohse, op. cit.; and Bernhard Lohse, "Reason and
Revelation in Luther," Scottish Journal of Theology,
XIII (1960), pp. 337-365.

   20. Lohse, "Reason and . . . ," pp. 344-345.
   21. Gerrish, op. cit., p. 10.
   22. See Harold J. Grimm, The Reformation Era
(New York: The Macmillan Co., 1965), pp. 61 ff.
   23. Ibid., p. 79. For a survey of Luther's
and Erasmus' relation to scholasticism see Pelikan,
From Luther . . . , pp. 5 ff.
   24. Fischer, op. cit., pp. 32-33. The work
Fischer summarizes is Hans Preuss, "Was bedeutet
die Formel Convictus testimoniis scripturarum aut
ratione evidente in Luthers ungehornter Antwort zu
Worms?", Theologische Studien und Kritiken 81 (Gotha:
Perthes, 1908), 62 ff. For a discussion of the
inherent ambiguity of "ratio" see Gerrish, op. cit.,
pp. 65 ff.
   25. Cranz, op. cit., p. 109.
   26. See A.E., I, 155 ff., (1535), where Luther
maintains that the Anabaptists and the Arians use
the same kind of misleading rationalization as did
Eve when she succumbed to the wiles of the serpent.

See also A.E., LI, 373 ff., (1546), where Luther, in his last sermon at Wittenberg, attacks the "fanatics" and, in this context, calls reason the "devil's whore." Throughout his Bondage of the Will, (1525), Luther sees no great power in the reasoning of Erasmus, but instead considers his opponent's so-called reasons as a series of misguided rationalizations born of a basic ignorance of the biblical message.

27. For a helpful summary of Luther's thought in this area see Whale, op. cit., pp. 34 ff., and Gerrish, op. cit., pp. 69-71. Cf. L.C.C., XV, 218-219, (1515-1516).

28. Lohse, "Reason and . . . ," p. 358. In this article Lohse pursues a helpful discussion of the thought of Occam, Biel, and Luther on the nature of the will and reason in natural man. I am much indebted to Lohse for material in this area.

29. Ibid., p. 359.

30. Luther follows William of Occam in this accent of the primacy of will over intellect. Cf. Copleston, op. cit., III/I, 113 ff. Note that Luther feels Erasmus has put his finger down on the crucial issue (Luther, Bondage . . . , p. 78).

31. Gerrish, op. cit., p. 72. Gerrish is interpreting material from W.A., XL/I, 291 ff.

32. A.E., XXVI, 174, (1531).

33. Cranz, op. cit., p. 106.

34. Jaroslav Pelikan, The Christian Intellectual (New York: Harper and Row, 1965), p. 58.

35. A.E., I, 48, and 41, (1535).

36. A.E., I, 31-32, (1535). This is not to imply that Luther's cosmology was cast in twentieth century terms. Certainly, as a man of his day, he believed a number of things about the nature of the world which we could not now accept. Furthermore, 16th century astronomy was deeply tinged with astrology. H. Grimm notes that Kepler himself "cast horoscopes for rulers, merchants, and mariners." (Grimm, op. cit., p. 588.) Cf. Charles Singer, A Short History of Scientific Ideas (Oxford Paperbacks: London: Oxford University Press, 1962), pp. 236 ff. According to Heinrich Boehmer, Martin Luther: Road to Reformation, trans. Doberstein and Tappert

("Living Age Books"; New York: Meridian Books, 1957),
p. vi, Luther looked upon astrology as a "scabby
art" while Melanchthon, in contrast, cast the horo-
scope of Luther several times.
    37. Gerrish, op. cit., p. 13.
    38. Lohse, "Reason and . . . ," p. 359.
    39. Heinrich Heine, Religion and Philosophy in
Germany, trans. John Snodgrass (Beacon Press Paperback: Boston: Beacon Press, 1959), pp. 50-51.
    40. Maritain, op. cit., p. 4.
    41. W.A., X/I/I, 527; as translated and quoted
by Gerrish, op. cit., p. 12.
    42. A.E., XXVI, 174-175, (1531).
    43. Luther, Bondage of . . . , p. 201, (1525).
    44. An excellent discussion of this problem is
to be found in Gerrish, op. cit., and in Lohse,
"Reason and . . . ." I am especially indebted to
Gerrish's work.
    45. Cf. Watson, op. cit., p. 7. Watson suggests
that we follow Luther's advice regarding an elementary
principle of interpretation. Commenting on Saint
Hilary's De Trinitate, Luther writes, "He who will
understand what is said must see why or for what
reasons it is said. Thus there are many sayings in
the Scriptures which, if taken literally, are
contradictory, but if the causes are shown, everything is right." Watson quotes from Martin Luther,
Works of Martin Luther (6 vols.: Philadelphia: A.
H. Holman Co., 1915-1932), V, p. 174. In the same
context Luther complains about those who collect
his "contradictions" without trying to understand
the reasons for them.
    46. Roland Bainton, The Reformation of the
Sixteenth Century (Beacon Press Paperback; Boston:
Beacon Press, 1956), p. 26. See Paul Tillich, The
Courage To Be (Yale Paperbound; New Haven: Yale
University Press, 1959), pp. 57 ff., for a development of the anxiety of guilt and condemnation which
characterized the end of the Middle Ages.
    47. See Watson, op. cit., pp. 15 ff. For an
extended discussion of Luther's decision to enter
a monastery see E. G. Schwiebert, Luther and His
Times (Saint Louis, Concordia Publishing House,
1950), pp. 136 ff.
    48. Watson, op. cit., p. 21.

49. <u>A.E.</u>, XXVI, 136, (1531).

50. <u>A.E.</u>, XXVI, 139, (1531).

51. <u>A.E.</u>, LI, 112, (1522). See also <u>A.E.</u>, XXVI, 126, and 131. Seeberg, <u>op. cit.</u>, vol. II, pp. 296 ff., discusses this centrality of focus in Luther.

52. Einar Billing, <u>Our Calling</u>, Conrad Bergendoff, trans. (Rock Island, Illinois: Augustana Book Concern, 1950), p. 7.

53. <u>A.E.</u>, XXII, 457-458, (1539).

54. <u>Ibid.</u>, p. 456.

55. <u>A.E.</u>, XXVI, 408-409, (1531).

56. <u>A.E.</u>, XXVII, 27, (1531).

57. <u>L.C.C.</u>, XV, 232, (1515-1516).

58. <u>A.E.</u>, LI, 112, (1522).

59. It should be noted that Luther does not simply identify God's "Word" with the Scriptures as such, as many studies have demonstrated. See, e.g.: Pinomaa, <u>op. cit.</u>, pp. 101-111; Watson, <u>op. cit.</u>, pp. 149-177; Rupp, <u>op. cit.</u>, pp. 320-322; and Jaroslav Pelikan, <u>A.E.</u>, Companion Volume, pp. 48-70. Rupp's summary is helpful: "Tt /the Word/ is for him a rich and many-sided complex, a master word which, . . . is not to be restricted to any one definition. It is the whole divine revelation, it is the revelation in Jesus Christ, it is the apostolic Kerugma, it is the living and preached Gospel, the whole witness of the Scriptures, mediated by the whole apparatus of institutional religion." (Rupp, <u>op. cit.</u>, p. 320.) The Word, then, is God's communication to men. This may come through the written Word, the Scriptures, or the preached Word in its oral form, or through the sacramental acts of the Church. This Word includes both Law and Gospel; but the heart of the content of the Word is Christ and the good news of God's grace known in and through him.

60. There are also two somewhat peripheral comments that Luther makes regarding the adequacy of natural reason in the realm of redemption. Several times he asserts that while reason is able to state what we <u>must</u> do, it in no way supplies the needed ability to do it (Cf. <u>A.E.</u>, II, 160). In another context Luther argues that if human reason were capable of grasping saving truth, then "it would not have been necessary for Christ to come

down from heaven with His revelation to us."
(A.E., XXII, 467.) To be sure, this argument tends
to be circular in that it seems to presuppose that
since Christ did come as revelation then men's
reason is not capable of grasping saving truth without such revelation.

61. A.E., XXVI, 113, (1531).
62. Gerrish, op. cit., p. vii.
63. A.E., LI, 373, (1546).
64. A.E., XXVI, 49 ff., (1531).
65. Gerrish, op. cit., pp. 116-117.
66. A.E., XXVI, 192, (1531). To be sure, some
have turned the charge of stubborness and presumption
against Luther; but we should note the norm of
Scripture which Luther suggests at this point.

67. In the reformation setting Luther's opposition
to Zwingli centered around the interpretation of the
Lord's Supper. Luther felt that Zwingli's rationalism
led the Swiss reformer to misinterpret the plain
meaning of the passage of Scripture where the Lord
instituted the Eucharistic celebration (See Grimm,
op. cit., pp. 193-195). On the other hand, Luther's
conflict with Thomas Munzer was rooted in Munzer's
conviction that the Holy Spirit spoke directly to
him and to others and thus the Bible, as such, could
be set aside as normative (Grimm, op. cit., pp.
172-173).

68. A.E., XXVI, 124, (1531). Gerrish notes
that the Nominalists, on the whole, insisted that
while some kind of merit was possible before grace,
nevertheless merit "in the strict sense required
the assistance of grace." (Gerrish, op. cit., pp.
121-122).

69. Gerrish, op. cit., pp. 124 ff. The following
is an all too brief summary of Gerrish's argument
on a highly complex and interesting problem.

70. Compare A. C. McGiffert, A History of
Christian Thought (2 vols.; Scribner paperback;
New York: Charles Scribner's Sons, 1965), II, p. 283.

71. A.E., XXVI, 146 (1531).
72. Cf. Gerrish, op. cit., p. 132.
73. A.E., XXVI, 125-126 (1531).
74. As Luther puts the case in his Disputations
Against Scholastic Theology of 1517 (L.C.C., XVI,

269-270): "43) It is a wrong thing to say that a man cannot become a theologian without Aristotle (against the generally accepted opinion.) 44) The truth is that a man cannot become a theologian unless he becomes one without Aristotle. . . . 50) In short, compared with the study of theology, the whole of Aristotle is as darkness is to light (against the scholastic theologians)."

75. This presentation is not to be construed as a justification of Luther's position as over against either Thomas or the Nominalists. What we want to indicate here is Luther's ground for his rejection of reason in the sphere of theology. For a well developed discussion of Luther's view of the relation between reason and theology see Gerrish, op. cit., pp. 57-137.

76. A.E., XXVI, 262 (1531).

77. A.E., XXVI, 263 (1531). It is interesting to note that Luther, in this section, consistently links this theological "right reason" with a "good will." This corresponds to our analysis of the plight of reason. If reason fails, theologically speaking, in natural man it is largely because it is a tool and servant of a distorted will which is, itself, in bondage. Thus if reason is to be "healed," rescued from bondage. Just as the "whole man" is in need of grace, even so the "whole man" is a recipient of healing grace.

78. Gerrish, op. cit., p. 81. Cf. Luther's, "For reason should first be illuminated by faith before it works." A.E., XXVI, 267-268, (1531), Cf. also A.E., XXVI, 265, 266, 238, 274, and 284, (1531).

79. A.E., XXVI, p. 284, (1531). Underlining is mine.

80. Luther, Bondage . . . , p. 67, (1525).

81. A.E., XXVI, 8, (1531). Underling is mine.

82. Ibid., p. 238.

83. For discussions of Luther's view of such "natural knowledge" sec: Gerrish, op. cit., pp. 100 ff.; Watson, op. cit., pp. 73 ff.; Lohse, "Reason and . . . ," pp. 355 ff.; John Baillie, Our Knowledge of God (Scribner paperback; New York: Charles Scribner's Sons, 1959), pp. 189 ff.; and Pelikan, From Luther . . . , pp. 21-23.

84. L.C.C., XV, 23, (1515-1516). The relationship of the "linguistic" argument used in the latter
part of this citation to the ontological argument
is an interesting point to ponder.
85. A.E., XXVI, 399, (1531).
86. A.E., XXII, 150, (1537).
87. A.E., I, 25, (1535). It should be noted
that some scholars see the hand of a Melanchthonian
editor in the sections of Luther's writings which
reflect this type of argument. Pelikan notes that
some have concluded that Luther's Lectures on Genesis
have been reworked by editors so that they would
better conform to the growing orthodoxy of second
generation Lutheran theologians. On the other hand
Pelikan, while conceding a need for some doubt
regarding the authenticity of such passages, feels
that such skepticism is too severe and that there is
no inherent reason why the early thought of the
"young Luther" should be taken as the final norm of
authenticity. See Pelikan's introduction, Ibid.,
pp. XI-XII.
88. A.E., XXVI, 396, (1531).
89. A.E., II, 42, (1535).
90. A.E., XXVI, 28-29, (1531).
91. Ibid., p. 238.
92. Ibid., p. 399.
93. A.E., XXII, 150, (1537).
94. Ibid., pp. 152-153.
95. A.E., XXVI, 400, (1531).
96. Ibid., pp. 395-396, 401.
97. Kostlin, op. cit., I, 321, and II, 433.
Some explicit statements by Luther include: "What
the Gospel teaches and shows me is a divine work
given to me by sheer grace; neither human reason
nor wisdom nor even the Law of God teaches this.
And I accept this gift by faith alone." A.E.,
XXVI, 73, (1531). "In the end only the Holy Spirit
from heaven above can create listeners and pupils
who accept this doctrine and believe that the Word
is God, . . . that He is also the Light who can
illumine all men . . . and that without this light
all is darkness." A.E., XXII, 8, (1537). See
also: A.E., LI, 111-12, (1522); A.E., XXII, 457,
(1539); and A.E., XXVI, 113-114, (1531).

116

98. See Lohse, "Reason and . . . ," pp. 355 ff.; and Watson, op. cit., pp. 78 ff.

99. A.E., XXXI, 344, (1520).

100. Ibid., p. 367.

101. Lohse, "Reason and . . . ," p. 351.

102. Whale, op. cit., p. 17.

103. For discussions of these aspects of Luther's thought see: Kostlin, op. cit., II, 275-309; Gerrish, op. cit., pp. 77-81; Althaus, op. cit., pp. 31-42; Pinomaa, op. cit., pp. 3-5; Watson, op. cit., pp. 102-148.

104. A.E., XXII, 156, (1537).

105. Ex. 33:20; Watson, op. cit., pp. 78 ff.; A.E., XXVI, 28, (1531).

106. A.E., I, 11, (1535). Here Luther wrestles with the concept of time as it relates to God and creation, and suggests that while time may be a category of our reason we cannot apply such a category to God. Therefore we should dismiss speculations about what lies "outside of or before time," and all the fanciful arguments about what God was doing "before there was any time." Nothing can be said about all this because "our mind cannot grasp what lies outside them. . . . It is folly to argue much about God outside and before time, because this is an effort to understand the Godhead without a covering, or the uncovered divine essence. Because this is impossible, God envelops Himself in His works in certain forms, as today He wraps Himself up in Baptism, in absolution, etc. If you should depart from these, you will get into an area where there is no measure, no space, no time, and into the merest nothing, concerning which, according to the philosopher, there can be no knowledge."

107. A.E., XXVI, 29, (1531).

108. Gerrish, op. cit., pp. 77-78. Cf. A.E., II, 43 and 45, (1536); A.E., XXVI, 28-30, (1531); A.E., I, 13-14, (1535); and Luther, Bondage of . . . , p. 170.

109. A.E., II, 48, (1536).

110. A.E., I, 49, (1535).

111. A.E., XVI, 29, (1531). An interesting question grows out of Luther's argument. If, as Luther says, man cannot fathom God's transcendent

nature and man cannot know God as He is in Himself,
then on what grounds does Luther assert that the
"majesty of God . . . is too much for the human
body and especially for the human mind to bear"?
(A.E., XXVI, 28.) John Baillie suggests there is a
weakness and an inconsistency in Luther at this
point (Baillie, op. cit., p. 196, n. 1). Baillie
writes: "If God is known to us only in His
humiliation, then how do we know that apart from
this humiliation His attributes are those of blinding
glory and majesty?" Luther himself might reply by
referring Dr. Baillie to Exodus 33:20--". . . for man
shall not see me and live." Or Luther could argue
that man's natural knowledge of God does have some
grasp of God's eternal power and glory (Romans 1:20),
just as Luther also certainly asserts that man has
a "moral" knowledge of God by nature. It is primarily
this moral knowledge which, when heightened, produces
despair and a horror of God in man.

112. L.C.C., XVI, pp. 290 ff. See theses 19
through 22. Baillie, op. cit., p. 193, asserts
that Luther is here plainly directing his polemic
against the scholastic theologians. "When Luther
condemns the theologia gloriae, he is condemning
precisely the kind of natural theology practiced
by St. Thomas--the attempt to reach God from 'the
things which are made.'"

113. W.A., XVI, 447, as quoted by Watson, op.
cit., p. 99, n. 52. This is certainly a bold
assertion of a "point of contact."

114. L.C.C., XV, 53, (1515-1516).

115. Pinomaa, op. cit., pp. 8-9. He cites a
section of Luther's Theses Concerning Faith and
Law to buttress this view. In the 42nd thesis
on Law Luther writes, "Briefly, it is necessary
either to despair when one understands the law,
but is ignorant of the grace of God, or, one must
trust in one's self, not understanding the law and
despising the wrath of God." A.E., XXXIV, 116-117,
(1535).

116. Seebert, op. cit., II, 247. Seeberg cites
Luther's lectures on Galatians of 1519. Here
Luther approves of Augustine's comments on Gal.
3:23, to the effect that man, through the Law, has

118

come to the knowledge of his illness; furthermore,
this knowledge has brought about a stronger desire
and a more ardent love for a physician. Commenting on the Old Testament fathers, Luther writes:
"For the same faith also came long ago to the
fathers, because the Law of God, when first
revealed to them, also compelled them to seek
grace." (A.E., XXVII, 277.)

117. A.E., XXVII, 284, (1519). Underlining
is mine.

118. A.E., XXVI, 327, (1531); See also p. 364,
lines 17-19.

119. Rupp, op. cit., p. 167.

120. A.E., XXVII, 56, (1531).

121. Ibid., p. 53.

122. A.E., XXII, 457-458, (1539). Cf. Ibid.,
p. 456.

123. Rupp, op. cit., p. 161.

124. L.C.C., XV, 81, (1515-1516).

125. A.E., XXXI, 346-347, (1520).

126. A.E., XXVI, 408-409. Compare a section
from Luther's sermons on John: "Through the only-
begotten Son and through the Gospel one learns to
look directly into God's face. And when this happens,
then everything in man dies; man must then confess
that he is a blind and ignorant sinner who must
forthwith appeal to Christ." A.E., XXII, 157, (1537).

127. Seeberg, op. cit., II, 229. This view is
consistent with the witness of the Christian saints
of all ages, for the greatest of saints have often
confessed themselves to be among the chief sinners
(I. Tim. 1:15). Reinhold Niebuhr makes this point
from another angle in his The Nature and Destiny
of Man (One volume edition; New York: Charles
Scribner's Sons, 1955), Vol. II, p. 75: "There are
ultimate problems of life which cannot be fully
stated until the answer to them is known. Without
the answer to them, men will not allow themselves
to contemplate the full depth of the problem, lest
they be driven to despair."

128. Johnson, op. cit., p. 124.

129. A.E., XXIV, 337, (1537).

130. A.E., XXXIV, 116, (1535).

131. Kostlin, op. cit., II, 498. He does not
cite the source for this quotation.

132. Regin Prenter, Spiritus Creator, trans. by
John Jensen (Paperback edition; Philadelphia: Muhlenberg Press, 1953), p. 7. Prenter gives a very helpful discussion of the role of the Holy Spirit in
bringing man to a clarity of self-knowledge in
pp. 3-27 of his work. For other comments by Luther
on this theme see: A.E., XXVI, 381 and 384, (1531);
and L.C.C., XV, 79, 81, 222, 223, 245, (1515-1516).
133. On these grounds Luther resists Johannes
Agricola's conviction that only the Gospel needs to
be preached. Cf. Kostlin, op. cit., II, 498; and
Grimm, op. cit., p. 231.
134. See Watson, op. cit., p. 17 ff., for Luther's
view on attritio and contritio. See Kostlin, op. cit.,
II, 499, for "Cain's repentance," and the "foothold"
metaphor.

CHAPTER V

THEOLOGY AND REASON: TILLICH

"Reason is the presupposition of faith, and
faith is the fulfillment of reason." Dynamics
of Faith, p. 77.

        While there may be some ambiguity in Luther's
attitude toward reason and philosophy, there is
little ambiguity in Paul Tillich's stance. Perhaps
the most striking statement from Tillich which reflects his view comes from that book in which he
seeks to demonstrate the inevitable link between
biblical religion and philosophy: "Against Pascal
I say: The God of Abraham, Isaac, and Jacob and
the God of the philosophers is the same God."[1]
Certainly this is not to say, as we shall show in
this chapter, that Tillich puts any final trust in
human reason as such, but his attitude toward reason
is obviously more consistently positive than is
Luther's. What, then, is Tillich's understanding of
the nature of reason and its place in the field of
theology?

        "Epistemology, the 'knowledge' of knowing,
is a part of ontology, the knowledge of being, for
knowing is an event within the totality of events.
Every epistemological assertion is implicitly
ontological."[2] In the light of that assertion,
Tillich concludes that the most adequate systematic
approach would be to begin with ontological considerations, with an analysis of existence and the
question of being rather than with a consideration
of the problems involved in knowing. Such was the
approach of the predominant classical tradition.
Yet there may be times, such as ours, when the order
needs to be reversed, since in such times the focus
comes to bear on the "how" of knowing because the
ontological tradition has come under suspicion.
With this weakening of the ontological tradition,
the question "arises whether the tools used in the
creation of this tradition are responsible for its
failure."[3] Since theology's path to knowledge seems

to deviate from the ordinary ways of knowing, theology, especially, must be prepared to give an account of how it knows that it knows. Thus Tillich's opening section of his major work is a consideration of reason.

While Tillich may begin with epistemological considerations, he insists that these do not provide the foundations for his theology. He observes that classical theology "has been aware that a doctrine of revelation presupposes doctrines of God, man, Christ, etc."[4] Thus part I of Systematic Theology, "Reason and the Quest for Revelation," is dependent on the whole system. As Tillich indicated earlier, theology should reflect a methodological rationality, yet it is not a "deductive" system in the sense that certain key axioms are sources from which one deduces the rest of Christian doctrine.[5] The system is organically interrelated rather than deductively structured.

Reflecting his consistent concern for semantic clarity, Tillich seeks to define "reason." To begin with, he distinguishes between an "ontological" and a "technical" concept of reason.[6] The ontological or "classical" understanding of reason is the dominant view from Parmenides to Hegel, while the technical view of reason has become dominant under the impact of English empiricism and the breakdown of German classical idealism. Tillich defines ontological reason as that "structure of the mind which enables the mind to grasp and to transform reality."[7] In this sense classical reason is logos, the rational structure of the universe in which man participates. This concept of reason would encompass the various functions of the human mind by which we find and express meaning and creativity. It is reflected not only in the cognitive activities, but also in the "aesthetic, practical, and technical functions of the human mind." The emotional life is part of this rational structure, as Plato suggested when he spoke of eros driving the mind toward the true, and as Aristotle indicated when he spoke of love for the perfect form as that

power which moves all things. Ontological reason
seems to refer to the whole of man as he lives in
creative interaction with his world. Reason, in
this sense, is

> . . . identical with the humanity of man in
> contrast to all other beings. It is the basis
> of language, of freedom, of creativity. It is
> involved in the search for knowledge, the exper-
> ience of art, the actualization of moral
> commands; it makes a centered personal life and
> a participation in community possible. [8]

On the other hand, the technical concept of
reason accompanies the ontological and sometimes
replaces it. Here "reason is reduced to the capacity
for 'reasoning.' Only the cognitive side of the
classical concept of reason remains, and within the
cognitive realm only those cognitive acts which
deal with the discovery of means for ends." [9] This
is reason as it is commonly expressed in scientific method, logical discipline, and technical cal-
culation. This is the type of reason which has been
so enormously successful in helping man to control
and direct his environment, although it must draw
from some other realm in order to speak of _ends_ for
the means which it devises. [10]

While Tillich recognizes the validity and
the narrow power of technical reason, he feels that
in itself it is inadequate as a total approach to
life. If ontological reason is denied its place
and technical reason rules the field, then the ends
for which man strives must be provided by "non-ra-
tional forces, either by positive traditions or by
arbitrary decisions serving the will to power." [11]
Meanings, values, and ends are grounded in a reality
which technical reason alone cannot discern. So
while technical reason "always has an important
function, even in systematic theology," it is
"adequate and meaningful only as an expression of
ontological reason and as its companion." Theology
need not decide between the two since both have
their place in the theological enterprise. Tillich's

own openness to the disciplines of historical studies and of biblical criticism is rooted in this basic acceptance of technical reason. Yet such disciplines are always only preliminary in terms of the final concerns of theology; they may function as an anti-septic--in the sense of destroying superstitions--but they "do not even touch faith." Reason, then, in its narrow and broad sense has its necessary place in theological activity. In order for man to be man he must express himself through reason; and while Tillich accepts revelation as a reality he never looks upon revelation as something which destroys reason or sets it aside. Indeed, "the command to sacrifice one's intellect is more demonic than divine. For man ceases to be man if he ceases to be an intellect."[12]

Theology discusses the relationship between reason and revelation not at the level of technical reason, but at the level of ontological reason, of "reason in the sense of logos." Technical reason, viewed as the tool that it is, is an instrument to be used more or less perfectly depending upon the skill of the reasoning person. On the other hand, ontological reason, as man experiences it, is involved in existential problems. Ontological reason, as it is actualized in the self and in the world, is involved in the "broken" aspects of existence; it is subjected to "finitude and separation." The healing of this reason does not depend upon technique, but upon a "saving" act of revelation. The traditional view of the brokenness of reason is expressed in Tillich's thought:

The religious judgment that reason is "blind," for instance, neither refers to technical reason, which can see most things in its own realm quite well, nor to ontological reason in its essential perfection, namely, in unity with being-itself. The judgment that reason is blind refers to reason under the conditions of existence; and the judgment that reason is weak--partly liberated from blindness, partly held in it--refers to reason within life and history.[13]

Another distinction Tillich makes in developing his concept of reason is that between "subjective" and "objective" reason. "Subjective reason
is the structure of the mind which enables it to
grasp and to shape reality on the basis of a
corresponding structure of reality."[14] This subjective reason is actualized in an individual self
and expresses itself by "penetrating" into the
"essential nature of a thing or an event," and by
"understanding and expressing" it. The acts of
"grasping" and "shaping" are interdependent, since
reality itself tends to be transformed by the way
we see it--to "know" truth is to "do" truth (John
3:21). Objective reason, on the other hand, is
the "rational structure of reality which the mind
can grasp and according to which it can shape
reality."[15] Subjective reason, reason in the individual self, relates to objective reason, the rational structure of the world in which the individual
participates. "Reason in the philosopher grasps
the reason in nature. Reason in the artist grasps
the meaning of things. Reason in the legislator
shapes society according to the structures of
social balance."[16]

The next aspect of reason which Tillich
considers is the "depth of reason." In his own
words, the

> depth of reason is the expression of something
> that is not reason but which precedes reason
> and is manifest through it. Reason in both
> its objective and its subjective structures
> points to something which appears in these
> structures but which transcends them in power
> and meaning.[17]

This "depth of reason" is neither a field in which
reason can be discovered and expressed nor an area
which reason can investigate or express directly.
Rather, this "depth of reason" is that which is itself expressed "through every rational expression."
Tillich writes:

It could be called the "substance" which appears

in the rational structure, or "being-itself"
which is manifest in the logos of being, or
the "abyss" which cannot be exhausted by any
creation or by any totality of them, or the
"infinite potentiality of being and meaning"
which pours into the rational structures of
the mind and reality, actualizing and transforming them.[18]

All the terms used in that quotation are terms
designed to function metaphorically and thereby
"point" to that which "precedes" reason. "Preceding"
is itself to be considered as a metaphorical expression. The point Tillich makes here is that, since
language works in the realm of reason and its
structures, one must use language symbolically if
one is to speak of that which is somehow "beyond"
(another metaphor) the structures of reason as such.
To put all this in more traditional language,
Tillich is simply saying that the "depth of reason"
is that quality of reason which points to God.[19]

        Although the depth of reason may be expressed
in reason, it is always hidden in reason under the
conditions of existence. This depth of reason,
which is not grasped or understood directly by
reason as we know it, is responsible for two
functions of the human mind which are not functions
of reason as such. These functions are myth and
cult. Tillich asserts that reason, in its essential
or "unfallen" nature, would not express itself in
myth and cult. But under the conditions of existence, actual reason has lost its immediate unity
with its own depth and thus is not "transparent" to
its depth. It is, rather, "opaque" and reflects the
depth of reason through myth and cult. In existence,
then, myth and cult serve a function which cannot be
derived from or reduced to the functions of reason
as such; nor can the rational character of myth and
cult be affirmed or denied. Myth and cult are to
be considered as "the expressions of the depth of
reason in symbolic form," and they "lie in a
dimension where no interference with the proper
functions of reason is possible."[20] There is no

basic conflict between myth and cult and reason, but
myth and cult prompt reason to raise the question of
revelation by pointing to that which lies beyond
the structures of reason.

While philosophy may talk of the essential
relation between man's reason and the rational
structure of reality as well as the "depth" of reason,
yet theology must ask whether the nature of reason
is not distorted in human existence. Does not man's
reason bear the scars of man's estrangement from his
essential self? Tillich is certainly aware of the
classical Christian assertion that man's reason is
also involved in the "fallen" nature of man. Reflecting on the biblical message, Tillich writes:

> Man is bound to sin in all parts of his being,
> because he is estranged from God in his person-
> al center. Neither his emotion, his will, nor
> his intellect is excepted from sin and, conse-
> quently, from the perversion of their true nature.
> His intellectual power is as distorted and weak
> ened as his moral power. . . . According to
> biblical religion, intellectual endeavor can as
> little attain the ultimate truth as moral end-
> eavor can attain the ultimate good. He who
> attempts it deepens the estrangement. This
> was the message of Paul, Augustine, Luther.[21]

Reflecting this position through his own terminology,
Tillich maintains that _actual_ reason, reason as we
know and use it, is involved in the finitude, the
self-destructive conflicts, and the ambiguities of
reality.[22] Both Nicolaus Cusanus with his principle
of "learned ignorance" and Immanuel Kant with his
"categories" reflect this finitude and limitations
of reason. Post-Kantian metaphysics fell into the
error of deifying reason; and when this deified
reason fell after Hegel, technical reason tended
to be enthroned in our time with the consequent
loss of "the universality and depth of ontological
reason."

Theology is justified in criticizing reason.
"But an accusation of reason _as_ _such_ is a symptom
either of theological ignorance or of theological

arrogance."[23] Actual reason has never completely
lost its basic structure since it is still rooted
in its creative ground. To lose completely its
basic structure would mean to cease to be; but to
be means to participate in the ground of being and
thus, to some degree, to express essential structure.
Theology correctly criticizes reason when theology
shows how reason, under the conditions of existence,
reflects the contradictions and disruptions of
existence through the various conflicts within
actual reason. "Under the conditions of existence
the structural elements of reason move against each
other. Although never completely separated, they
fall into self-destructive conflicts. . . ."[24]

     In its essential structure reason unites its
various elements or, in other words, establishes a
type of harmony between the various polar elements.
But reason in existence finds these elements in conflict with each other. Thus the polarity between
the structure and depth of reason results in a
conflict between autonomy and heteronomy. The
individual seeks to be obedient to the law of reason he finds within himself (autonomy), or he submits to an outer structure of law imposed upon him
(heteronomy). The static and dynamic poles in reason result in a tension between absolutism and
relativism. The absolutist position tends to identify truth and reason with certain special moral
or political forms, or aesthetic and philosophical
principles, while the relativist view, reflecting
the dynamic aspect of reason, tends to call all
patterns into question through the vitality of life
processes. Finally the formal and the emotional
elements of reason come into conflict. The former
accents the controlling side of knowledge and sees
formalized logic as the proper pattern for anything
which can legitimately be called knowledge. While
the emotional element (eros), senses that pure
formalism can destroy meaning and thus reacts in
the name of vitality and creativity.[25] These
conflicts within reason move reason to a quest for
revelation. "Reason does not resist revelation.
It asks for revelation, for revelation means the

integration of reason."[26]

    With this brief summary of the meaning and
structure of reason, as Tillich sees it, we turn
now to a consideration of philosophy as a major
expression of reason in human existence. In Chapter
II it was noted that Tillich has chosen to define
philosophy as that "cognitive approach to reality
in which reality as such is the object," or "that
cognitive endeavor in which the question of being is
asked." Philosophy involves, centrally, ontology
since it deals with the question of the meaning of
being, with the question of why there is something
and not nothing, and with the question of the structure
of being in which every being participates. Philosophy seeks to lay bare those structures which make
experience itself possible. In this sense philosophy
is an inevitable part of being human. A lengthy
quote catches this theme:

    Philosophy . . . is not a matter of liking or
    disliking. It is a matter of man as man, for
    man is that being who asks the question of
    being. Therefore, every human being philos-
    ophizes, just as every human being moralizes
    and acts politically, artistically, scientif-
    ically, religiously. . . . The child's rest-
    less question, "Why is this so; why is that
    not so?" and Kant's grandiose description,
    . . . of the God who asks himself, "Why am I?"
    are the same in substance although infinitely
    distinguished in form. Man is by nature a
    philosopher, because he inescapably asks the
    question of being. He does it in myth and
    epic, in drama and poetry, in the structures
    and the vocabulary of any language.[27]

Expressing this inevitability of philosophy in a
more existential mode, he writes: "We philosophize
because we are finite and because we know that we
are finite."[28]

    Philosophy's special task is to "make this
question /of being/ conscious and to elaborate the

answers methodologically." This attempt can be traced through the long history of philosophy and pre-philosophy. Though there are despisers of philosophy, they are hoist on their own petard since they must inevitably use language which has long been an expression and a product of philosophic endeavor. "We cannot avoid philosophy, because the ways we take to avoid it are carved out and paved by philosophy."[29]

So not only is the theologian inevitably involved in philosophy since, as a man, he asks the question of being; he is involved also because much of the language a theologian uses is dependent upon philosophic reflection for its meaning. The fundamentalist who would dispense with philosophy since Christians have "truth through revelation" does not realize that his very words "truth" and "revelation" are themselves products of philosophical reflection. Nor is a more sophisticated attempt at avoiding the use of philosophical terms in theology feasible.

It is my conviction that this is neither possible nor desirable and that the attempt to do it leads to self-deception and primitivism. In contrast . . . I try to show that each of the biblical symbols drives inescapably to an ontological question and that the answers given by theology necessarily contain ontological elements.[30]

In another work he makes much the same point:

Metaphysics cannot be avoided in any theology. For in order to interpret religious symbols, theology must use concepts which are either taken directly from a metaphysical system or which have already entered the general language without normally reminding of their philosophical origin.[31]

If every man, including the theologian, must be at least a crypto-philosopher, it seems fair to ask what the relation between philosophy and theology, as formal disciplines, might be.

Before exploring the positive relations between the
two disciplines, the distinctions should first be
elaborated. Put briefly, "Philosophy deals with
the structure of being in itself; theology deals
with the meaning of being for us."[32] This distinction
implies that there is a difference in the cognitive
attitudes. The philosopher, while driven by a
passion for truth, seeks to maintain an attitude of
detached objectivity toward being and its structures.
He tries to exclude all those elements which might
destroy an objective vision of reality. "In all
these respects he feels no different from the
scientist, historian, psychologist, etc. He col-
laborates with them." Indeed the sciences provide
much of the material which the philosopher uses
for his critical analysis of reality. Just as

> all the sciences have their origin in philosophy,
> so they contribute in turn to philosophy by
> giving to the philosopher new and exactly defined
> material . . . . This relation to the sciences
> (in the broad sense of Wissenschaften) strengthens
> the detached, objective attitude of the philos-
> opher.[33]

On the other hand the theologian is not
detached from his object, but is involved in it.

> The basic attitude of the theologian is a
> commitment to the content he expounds. Detach-
> ment would be a denial of the very nature of
> this content. The attitude of the theologian
> is "existential." He is involved--with the
> whole of his existence, . . . The theologian,
> in short, is determined by his faith.[34]

This involved attitude is in keeping with the first
formal criterion of theology as elaborated in
Chapter II of this work: "The object of theology
is what concerns us ultimately. Only those
propositions are theological which deal with their
object insofar as it can become a matter of ultimate concern for us." To be ultimately concerned
is to be grasped in one's totality by the object

131

of this concern, and to be so concerned is to be involved subjectively. The circle in which the theologian works is described by this ultimate concern. The theologian deals with the sciences only insofar as certain philosophical implications are at stake. He relates directly to the sciences in his philosopher's role, but not in his role as theologian. Theology deals with ultimate, philosophy with non-ultimate concerns. To look at reality "objectively" is not to be ultimately concerned, and thus such objectivity is not a theological stance.

Philosophy can also be distinguished from theology in terms of their respective sources.[35] The philosopher seeks to understand the structure of reality by looking at the whole of reality. He assumes some kind of identity, or at least analogy, between "objective and subjective reason," between the structures of reality and the forms of his own thought processes. The _logos_ in him has some distinct relation to the _logos_ of the reality he confronts. The object of his analysis is the whole of reality since "there is no particular place to discover the structure of being;" and "there is no particular place to stand to discover the categories of experience." The philosopher's stance is in "pure reason," which is not any particular place or view at all. On the other hand the theologian has a definite object of concern; thus he must "look where that which concerns him ultimately is manifest, and he must stand where its manifestation reaches and grasps him." The Christian theologian, then, finds his source of theological knowledge not in the universal _logos_ but in the Logos "who became flesh," the _logos_ as it has manifested itself in a "particular historical event." Since this is an event which precedes the history of the theologian, he must receive this manifestation through some medium. This medium is the church with its traditions and present reality; the medium is not the common rationality or experience of man.

A third distinction between theology and philosophy is to be found in their "content."[36]

Even in speaking about the same object they speak about something different. Both the philosopher and the theologian deal with the categories of being, with time, space, substance, and causality. But the philosopher relates these considerations to "the material which is structured by them." What Tillich seems to be saying is that the philosopher moves in a "horizontal dimension," he relates the categories of being to the world of reality, the phenomenological world around him which he directly confronts. In contrast the theologian relates the same categories and concepts to a soteriological quest. He makes assertions about the saving characteristics of the creative ground of life as it relates to life, rather than assertions only about the characteristics of life as it confronts us in actuality. The theologian is concerned primarily not about how reality is structured but about how reality as we know it might be and is redeemed under the power of the "New Being."

But while the formal disciplines of theology and philosophy may have clear distinctions, there is also an equally obvious convergence between them insofar as the man who exercises the disciplines is concerned.[37] Both philosopher and theologian, as men, exist; and both are conditioned by their psychological, sociological, and historical situation. Both, like every other human being, "exist in the power of an ultimate concern, whether or not he is fully conscious of it, whether or not he admits it to himself and to others." What Tillich is asserting, of course, is that everyman is implicitly a theologian in that everyman lives out of some type of ultimate concern. So while there may be a distinction between the formal disciplines of philosophy and theology, yet every "creative philosopher is a hidden theologian (sometimes even a declared theologian). He is a theologian in the degree to which his existential situation and his ultimate concern shape his philosophical vision."[38] The philosopher is a theologian to the degree that he understands the whole of reality in the light of some particular manifestation of reality which is given to him, and to the degree in which the particular manifestation becomes for him an ultimate concern. Thus we can find overt or hidden theologians of Nationalism, Racism, or Scientism, to name but a few possible idolatries. Just as, in Tillich's terms, every man is "religious," though not necessarily Christian, even so every man can be a "theologian" without being a Christian theologian.[39]

Actually, Tillich sees the philosopher and the theologian as bearing analogous burdens. The philosopher, while he has his particular commitments, tries to sustain an objective stance and thus keep the universal character of philosophy. Conversely the Theologian, while confessing and affirming his commitment, seeks to make clear the universal validity of that which does concern him ultimately. This means, says Tillich, that the theologian must seek for an attitude of detachment from his existential situation in order to be genuinely critical of "every special expression of his ultimate concern."[40] This detachment carries with it the risk of being driven beyond the boundary of the theological circle; in short, it can destroy the necessary element of involvement in the faith. It also means that the theologian cannot just repeat the affirmations of past generations; he "cannot join the chorus of those who live in unbroken assertions." He lives on the boundary of doubt and faith, or in that stance where doubt and faith exist together. "This tension is the burden and the greatness of every theological work."[41]

Posing the question of a possible conflict between or synthesis of philosophy and theology, Tillich asserts that a conflict is not necessary nor is a synthesis possible. "A conflict presupposes a common basis on which to fight. But there is no common basis between theology and philosophy. If the theologian and the philosopher fight, they do so on a philosophical or on a theological basis."[42] A fight may develop over

134

the ontological analysis of the structure of being, but this is a battle on the basis of pure reason, a battle of philosophy.

> The theologian has no right whatsoever to argue for a philosophical opinion in the name of his ultimate concern or on the basis of the theological circle. . . . It is a disgrace for the theologian and intolerable for the philosopher if in a philosophical discussion the theologian suddenly claims an authority other than pure reason.[43]

Perhaps the conflict most often involves a battle on the theological level. "The hidden theologian in the philosopher fights with the professed theologian." In this situation the philosopher, while seeking to be honest, is reluctant to admit to the "existentially conditioned element" in his system. He feels that personal commitment diminishes the truth value of his assertions and thus does not care to recognize that such commitments are, in fact, there. To cast this situation in other terms, when two such men battle as philosophers the goal is to convince; but when two such men compete as theologians, hidden or otherwise, the goal is to convert. So while our two contenders, one a philosopher and one a theologian, may battle either as philosophers or theologians, there is no conflict between their philosophy and their theology as such since there is no common basis.[44]

Given this lack of a common basis, neither can there be a synthesis of philosophy and theology. There is no possibility of structuring a "Christian philosophy," since this would kill the drive of philosophy by insisting that the philosopher adopt the concepts of some philosophic saint in the past, or by demanding that philosophy should develop under special conditions and with a special aim. In either situation the philosopher is barred from free and creative interaction of his reason with reality. "There is nothing in heaven and earth, or beyond them, to which the philosopher must subject himself

135

except the universal <u>logos</u> of being as it gives itself to him in experience."[45] At the same time Christianity does not need a "Christian" philosophy since it makes the claim, as a faith judgment, that the "Logos who has become concrete in Jesus as the Christ is at the same time the universal <u>logos</u>. . . ." This implies that wherever the <u>logos</u> is at work it agrees with the Christian message. It would seem strange, then, that a Christian should feel compelled to prove philosophically that which he accepts as part of his faith judgment--as part of the ultimate concern which grasps him.

Let us now look more closely at Tillich's <u>use</u> of reason and at how he envisages the role of reason in the first step of his Method--that of the raising of the questions. Put in another way, we must ask what the role of reason might be in delineating the human dilemma. How does reason help us to ascertain the "conflicts" of reason in existence which prompt men to ask for revelation? How does reason show man the nature of his finitude and thus prompt the question of God? How does reason develop such an understanding of man's existential estrangement, of the ambiguities of life, of the problem of history itself that man is prepared for the revealed answers of the New Being in Jesus as the Christ, the healing work of the divine Spirit, and the vision of the Kingdom of God? What we attempt at this point is not a summary of Tillich's own detailed analyses of these various "questions," but an outline of the assumptions and procedures which lie behind these analyses.

While a veritable multitude of strands of Western philosophy seem to meet and mix in Tillich's thought, Bernard Martin accurately observes that Heidegger and Husserl are the two modern German philosophers to whom Tillich is most indebted.[46] Much of Tillich's conception of the nature of philosophical reflection is tied to Husserl's phenomenology. From this stance the task of the philosopher is seen to be that of analyzing, disinterestedly, "basic 'essences' or 'structures'

136

given in experience to human consciousness while
'bracketing' the question of the particular
existence of the knower and the objects known."[47]
But, as both Martin and Cobb point out, Tillich's
own philosophy moves beyond the limits of pure
phenomenology and ventures into inferences which
are not warranted by phenomenology alone.[48] Cobb
states, "Tillich himself includes both phenomenological and inferential elements within ontology."
While Tillich feels that phenomenology is helpful
in clarifying certain notions, he also contends
that reason can range beyond such descriptions and
investigate the structure of reality itself. The
philosopher seeks, through his reason, to grasp
the rational structure of reality. "The philosopher
looks at the whole of reality to discover within
it the structure of reality as a whole. He tries
to penetrate into the structures of being by means
of the power of his cognitive function and its
structures."[49]

The phenomenological side of Tillich's
thinking is expressed in a number of important areas
of his thought. Two central examples would be his
phenomenological account of faith, and his explication
of the characteristics of estrangement in human
existence.[50] With the formal definition of faith
as "ultimate concern," Tillich sees faith as a universal phenomenon central to man's personal life.
Faith is not the property of Christian experience
alone, but of human experience generally insofar
as man exhibits ultimate concerns. Therefore faith
can be analyzed phenomenologically. Through his
analysis Tillich seeks to show that "there is a
quality of ultimate concern that characterizes all
those who are serious about life, regardless of
the end to which they may give themselves."[51] In
much the same manner estrangement is seen as an
aspect of general human experience and is, therefore,
an open field for phenomenological analysis.
Tillich's The Courage To Be is a work which reflects
such an analysis. Here Tillich sees human existence
threatened by three fundamental forms of anxiety.
Ontic anxiety grows out of man's awareness of his

radical contingency; for man knows that while he
is, he might also not be and someday will not be.
Moral anxiety grows out of the split which man
experiences between what he is and what his ideal
possibilities are. Man is not what he would be,
thus he finds himself guilty. Finally spiritual
anxiety results from the experience of emptiness
and meaninglessness in life. Man is, but he finds
no meaning for his existence. These various anxieties
are aspects of man's sense of estrangement from his
essential self and from the ground of his being,
and can be spelled out through phenomenological
analysis.

The more specifically ontological analyses
in Tillich's thought are tied to what might be seen
as a major stream in Western thought which ranges
from the pre-Socratics to the German idealists, and
especially Schelling.[52] Tillich finds certain
features of this tradition indispensible to philosophical reflection, and in so doing Tillich admittedly moves beyond the stringent limitations of much
contemporary Anglo-Saxon philosophy. Tillich's
ontological analysis moves beyond the descriptive
task of phenomenology into an area of inferences
about the nature of reality. Phenomenology may
point to these ontological concepts but it cannot
describe them.

The basic ontological structure which Tillich
discerns is the self-world or subject-object structure
of reality, and it is this subject-object structure
which is the basis for all thought. Man finds himself as a self within a world. As subject man relates
to objects.

Man experiences himself as having a world to
which he belongs. . . . Self-relatedness is
implied in every experience. There is something that "has" and something that is "had,"
and the two are one. The question is not
whether selves exist. . . . A self is not a
thing that may or may not exist; it is an
original phenomenon which logically precedes
all questions of existence.[53]

138

Man, as a subject, is never a "thing" since he is, as a self, a bearer of subjectivity. Yet no "thing" is completely devoid of subjectivity, not even a tool.

> Everything resists the fate of being considered or treated as a mere thing, as an object which has no subjectivity. This is the reason why ontology cannot begin with things and try to derive the structure of reality from them. That which is completely conditioned, which has no selfhood and subjectivity, cannot explain self and subject.[54]

In addition to this subject-object correlation, which is the "basic ontological structure," Tillich finds three other levels of ontological concepts. These include 1) polar elements which constitute the ontological structure: Individuality and universality, dynamics and form, freedom and destiny; 2) the characteristics of finitude—of being under the conditions of existence; 3) the categories of being and knowing: time, space, causality, and substance.[55]

Our major concern, here, is not so much with the adequacy of Tillich's philosophical stance—a much debated topic, to be sure—but with the assumptions which are involved in this stance and the various possible implications for theology.[56] Tillich follows in that "old tradition" which holds that "the principles which constitute the universe must be sought in man. . . ."[57] Man's being is the key to the nature of being in general.

> Man occupies a pre-eminent position in ontology, not as an outstanding object among other objects, but as that being who asks the ontological question and in whose self-awareness the ontological answer can be found. . . . Man is able to answer the ontological question himself because he experiences directly and immediately the structure of being and its elements.[58]

Thus when man analyzes the structures which make his own experience possible, the results apply not merely to man's being, but to all beings, at least by analogy.[59]

The centrality of man in the ontological enterprise is stated in another form when Tillich refers to man as microcosmos. Man is not distinct from or independent of his environment and world, rather he participates in his world. This insight has led philosophers like Cusanus and Leibniz to assert "that the whole universe is present in every individual, although limited by its individual limitations."[60] In Tillich's monism all beings reflect, to some degree, the world in which they participate. Thus every being has microcosmic qualities.

> But man alone is microcosmos. In him the world is present not only indirectly and unconsciously but directly and in a conscious encounter. Man participates in the universe through the rational structure of mind and reality. . . . Considered cosmically, he participates in the universe because the universal structures, forms, and laws are open to him. . . . The universals make man universal; language proves that he is microcosmos. Through the universals man participates in the remotest stars and the remotest past. This is the ontological basis for the assertion that knowledge is union and that it is rooted in the eros which reunites elements which essentially belong to each other.[61]

This brief overview has been designed to show that Tillich's philosophic side is shaped by an interest in phenomenological method and ontological analysis. His ontology, which indicates the structures of reality, tends to complement his phenomenology, which describes the reality presented to man. It is out of this broad philosophic stance that Tillich describes man's existential situation and lays the ground for the existential questions.

A key aspect of the philosophic stance is Tillich's broad concern for those aspects of culture which reflect man's spirit and which, thereby, speak most clearly of man's existential situation--of man's fears and hopes, man's joys and anxieties. Tillich draws on such areas as art, science, and literature for his analysis, though he finds that the most sensitive and creative expressions of man's cultural and spiritual life in the first half of the twentieth century are to be found in the "great works of visual arts, of music, of poetry, of literature, of architecture, of dance, /and/ of philosophy."[62] These various expressions represent the key to contemporary culture, a key to the nature of man's predicament "both in the present world and in the world universally." Existentialist thought and depth psychology are two particularly powerful expressions of man's situation, and they also provide avenues for the understanding of man's situation.

> Both existentialism and depth psychology are interested in the description of man's existential predicament. . . . The focus in both . . . is man's estranged existence, the characteristics and symptoms of this estrangement, and the conditions of existence in time and space.[63]

In an article on pastoral psychology, Tillich goes so far as to state: "It is an astonishing fact that Protestant theology had to rediscover its own tradition about what man is, and about what healing powers are, through the impact of the psychology of the unconscious."[64] Tillich sums up the role of such cultural factors for his system in this way:

> The material of the existential question is taken from the whole of human experience and its manifold ways of expression. This refers to past and present, to popular language and great literature, to art and philosophy, to science and psychology. It refers to myth and liturgy, to religious traditions, and to

141

present experiences. All this, as far as it
reflects man's existential predicament, is the
material without the help of which the existential question cannot be formulated.[65]

According to the Method, then, Tillich
proposes to raise the existential questions with
the help of an analysis which involves phenomenology
and ontology. For example, an analysis of man's
essential nature, which involves a consideration
of man's finitude, implies a question which corre-
lates to the theological answer of "God" (part II
of the system). And an analysis of man's existential self-estrangement implies a question which is
answered by the Christian message of "the Christ"
(part III of the system).

In what sense, we must now ask, are these
"existential questions," which are posed by the
Method, universal human questions? Or should they
be seen as questions which belong to a particular
type of human existence or a particular understanding
of human existence? This type of question is raised
by those critics of Tillich who share a more
Barthian outlook on the theological enterprise.
Alexander McKelway asks if the questions which
Tillich raises are "really man's questions."[66]
Robert Johnson writes that in Tillich's method
"there is no assurance or guarantees that the
questions with which Christian theology deals are
Christian questions--and even less that they are
the Christian questions."[67] While from another
point of view, Harvey Cox dismisses Tillich's
approach since Cox's "urban-secular" man is closed
to the ultimate or existential questions which
Tillich feels man must, by his very nature, ask.[68]

In an essay dealing with the communication
of the Christian message, Tillich expresses the
conviction that the questions which he seeks to
raise are, in fact, universal questions. In
addressing that man who feels that the Christian
Gospel does not speak to his condition, the theologian should first seek to

142

communicate the Gospel as a message of man
understanding his own predicament. What we
must do, and can do successfully, is to show
the structures of anxiety, of conflicts, of
guilt. These structures, which are effective
because they mirror what we are, are in us,
and if we are right, they are in other people
also.[69]

In another context Tillich asserts the universality
of the search for ultimate reality:

It is our finitude in interdependence with
the finitude of our world which drives us to
search for ultimate reality. This search is
a consequence of our encounter as finite
beings with a finite world. Because we stand
between being and nonbeing and long for a form
of being that prevails against nonbeing in
ourselves and in our world, we philosophize.[70]

While in his major work he writes: "The question,
asked by man, is man himself. He asks it, whether
or not he is vocal about it. He cannot avoid
asking it, because his very being is the question
of his existence."[71]

Such quotations seem to be in keeping with
the general thrust of Tillich's description of his
Method. Yet there is another side to this matter
which deserves close attention because it puts the
Method itself in a different light. There are
explicit statements from Tillich which indicate
that the particular questions raised through his
analysis may, after all, be questions which some
people are not in position to ask. At one point
Tillich indicates that persons who have participated
in other religio-cultural traditions may not be
"open" to the kinds of questions which the Gospel
seeks to answer.

The difficulty with the highly developed
religions of Asia, for instance, is not
so much that they reject the Christian
answer as answer, as that their human nature

143

is formed in such a way that they do not ask the questions to which the Gospel gives the answer. To them the Christian answer is no answer because they have not asked the question to which Christianity is supposed to give the answer.[72]

That the existential questions raised in the system may not be an inherent part of human experience is also implied in Tillich's comments regarding Christian education. In elaborating on two principles which should be followed in the religious education of children, Tillich writes:

The first is that the questions which are really in the hearts of the children should be answered and the children should be shown that the Biblical symbols and the Christian message are an answer to just these questions. And, secondly, we ought to seek to shape their existence in the direction of the questions which we believe are the more universal ones. This would be similar to what we do with the primitive peoples in the mission field. We seek to answer their questions and in doing so we, at the same time, slowly transform their existence so that they come to ask the questions to which the Christian message gives the answer.[73]

In another context Tillich asserts:

Religious education mediates a material which cannot be received by the mind of those who have not asked the questions to which these words give answers. These words are like stones, thrown at them, from which sooner or later they must turn away. Therefore, every religious educator must try to find the existentially important questions which are alive in the minds and hearts of the pupils. It must make the pupil aware of the questions which he already has.[74]

The implication of such comments would seem to be

that the "questions" which Tillich would pose in
his system may not be the questions which persons
in other cultures or at other levels of maturity
find compelling. Yet these persons can be brought
to another level of "asking" or of maturity so that
they will, in their "transformed" existence, find
the Christian answers applicable to their new
questions.

All of this poses further questions. Are
the "existential questions" developed by reason
alone? Are they abstracted from the general human
situation in which all human beings participate on
the basis of their common humanity? Or are there,
in fact, some preconditions which are involved before the questions can actually be raised? The
quotations just cited tend to indicate that a person needs to bear the imprint of a certain religio-
cultural tradition--by way of education in his own
culture, or mission work in another--before the
existential questions will, in fact, become his
questions. Such an interpretation would certainly
be consistent with Tillich's understanding of the
intimate relation between religion and culture,
and, therefore, his understanding of the intimate
relationship between an individual's spiritual
life and that individual's culture. Every human
being is conditioned, to no small degree, by the
cultural milieu in which he has matured. This is
one of the implications of the self-world polarity
which Tillich sees as central in his ontology.
Tillich expresses this tie between religion, person,
and culture in this manner:

> Religion as ultimate concern is the meaning-
> giving substance of culture, and culture is
> the totality of the forms in which the basic
> concern of religion expresses itself. In
> abbreviation: religion is the substance of
> culture, culture is the form of religion. . . .
> Every religious act, not only in organized
> religion, but also in the most intimate move-
> ment of the soul, is culturally formed.[5]

Thus, religiously speaking, it would follow that the "questions" which a person will ask are shaped to some degree by the environment which shapes the person. Indeed, it would seem that the religious "answers" which have constituted the substance of a culture would have much to do with the kind of questions raised within that culture. Primitive peoples, for instance, with a deep sense of corporate personality would hardly claim the existential questions raised by a modern French individualist-existentialist as his own questions.

Not only does the cultural setting shape the questions which a man will raise about himself and his existence, but it also shapes the philosophic side of the man within that culture.

No philosopher living within Western Christian culture can deny his dependence on it /historical Christianity/, as no Greek philosopher could have hidden his dependence on an Apollonian-Dionysian culture, even if he was a radical critic of the gods of Homer. The modern vision of reality and its philosophical analysis is different from that of pre-Christian times, whether one is or is not existentially determined by the God of Mount Zion and the Christ of Mount Golgotha. Reality is encountered differently; experience has different dimensions and directions than in the cultural climate of Greece. No one is able to jump out of this "magic" circle.[76]

This system of "feed-back," as we might call it, which operates within the complex of culture, religion, and person is expressed in more explicitly theological terms in Tillich's thought. Let us present a number of quotations for analysis:

But dialectic thinking maintains that the question about the divine possibility is a human possibility. And, further, it maintains that no question could be asked about the divine possibility unless a divine answer, even if preliminary and scarcely intelligible,

146

were not always already available. For in
order to be able to ask about God, man must
already have experienced God as the goal of
a possible question. Thus the human possibility of the question is no longer purely a
human possibility, since it already contains
answers.[77]

Nobody is able to ask questions concerning God,
revelation, Christ, etc., who has not already
received some answer.[78]

Symbolically speaking, God answers man's
questions, and under the impact of God's
answers man asks them.[79]

Man, in relation to God, cannot do anything
without him. He must receive in order to act.
New being precedes new acting. The tree produces the fruits, not the fruits the trees.[80]

The most straightforward interpretation of these
sections would seem to necessitate the conclusion
that the existential questions are never raised in
the total absence of the answers. Rather the
ability to raise the questions is, itself, dependent
upon some type of previous encounter with the answers.
This relationship between question and answer takes
on the characteristics of the many "polar" aspects
in Tillich's thought. Question and answer are in
polar relation in that while each possess their
own identity, yet they are interdependent in the
sense that one needs the other for its own reality.
The answers are not answers unless the questions
are asked, and the questions cannot be asked unless
some semblance of the answer is already given. This
view of an interdependent relationship between questions and answers is systematically compatible with
Tillich's understanding of the "history of revelation."

The event which is called "final revelation"
was not an isolated event. It presupposed a
revelatory history which was a preparation
for it and in which it was received. It could

147

not have occurred without having been expected,
and it could not have been expected if it had
not been preceded by other revelations which
had become distorted.[81]

. . . .

Only on the wide basis of universal revelation
could the final revelation occur and be
received. Without the symbols created by
universal revelation the final revelation would
not be understandable. Without the religious
experiences created by universal revelation
no categories and forms would exist to receive
the final revelation.[82]

The final revelation, Jesus as the Christ, is
received as "revelation"--as a healing answer--only
because preparatory revelations had prepared the
ground for the Christ event and its reception. The
way for the ultimate answer has been prepared by
penultimate answers. In like manner the way for
the asking of the existential questions was prepared
by answers which had earlier been fed into the stream
of spiritual history.

To put these considerations in other terms,
it seems that an act of grace not only precedes
the raising of the questions but also grants the
possibility of raising the questions. Indeed at
points Tillich turns to more orthodox terminology
and speaks of the role which the Holy Spirit plays
in man's understanding of his dilemma. God Himself
acts so that man becomes aware of his predicament;
and this awareness itself is a sign of the preparatory
work of God. This perspective is reflected in the
following passages:

He /any person/ may experience revelation at
his own condemnation. . . . As Luther frequently
emphasized, the feeling of being rejected is
the first and decisive step toward salvation;
. . . Neither sin nor despair, as such, proves
the absence of saving power. The absence of
saving power is expressed in the flight from
an ultimate concern and in the type of
complacency which resists both the shaking

148

experience of revelation and the transforming
experience of salvation.[83]

In the moment when we feel separated from God,
meaningless in our lives, and condemned to
despair, we are not left alone. The Spirit,
sighing and longing in us and with us, represents
us. It manifests what we really are. . . .
Those outside that experience possess nothing.[84]

There is no easy way of making men aware of
their predicament. God, certainly, has His
ways of doing so. He shakes the complacency
of those who consider themselves whole by
throwing them into darkness and despair,
externally and internally. He reveals to them
what they are by undercutting the foundations
of their self-assurance. He reveals their
blindness about themselves. We cannot do this,
not even with ourselves.[85]

We must conclude, then, that the existential
questions, for which the Christian message provides
the answers, is not raised by pure reason in the
sense of being abstracted from general human experience. Rather, the questions are raised from within the context of historical and personal situations
which have been "graced" by preparatory revelation
and which have been, therefore, prepared to educe
those questions which the Christian message, in
its ultimacy, will answer. "Symbolically speaking,
God answers man's questions, and under the impact
of God's answers man asks them."[86] That man must
ask about the infinite to which he belongs indicates
that man is estranged from it; that man can ask is
an indication that he is still essentially rooted
in the divine ground.

A question might naturally be posed at this
point. Does not this intimate interrelation of
question and answer tend to vitiate the distinction
between them and thus undercut the Method itself?
Tillich is sensitive to the question and suggests
this answer in one context:

149

I fully agree . . . that no "nice division"
between existential questions and theological
answers is possible . . . because the nature
of the method itself makes it impossible.
Questions and answers determine each other in
a definable way. And in the case of the
theologian, both lie within the "theological
circle" which is characterized by this interdependence. Nevertheless, the points of
approach are different in the case of the
question (the description of man's nature and
predicament) and the answer (the way of living
with one's finitude or the way of overcoming
one's predicament).[87]

Beyond this response some other considerations can
be offered. While Tillich would hold that his
Method has universal formal application, he certainly conceives of his task as that of being an
apologetic theologian within the context of
Western culture. More specifically, Tillich is
concerned primarily about reaching "modern" man--
meaning not all those who exist within the time
span of current history, but those who represent
the leading edge of the cultural-spiritual situation.
The artists, poets, and existentialist philosophers
are among those who participate most deeply in this
"modern" situation. The "questions" which Tillich
would raise, then, are questions which would parallel
the vision and experience of these modern men.
Tillich is primarily concerned that these men might
see the meaning of the Christian answer. Since
Tillich seeks to speak to a certain group of men
within a special historical context, "questions and
answers" must "determine each other" in order to
make living contact with such men in their situation.
In this sense, apologetic theology is always
contextual.[88]

        The inherent interrelation between question
and answer is implied, furthermore, when Tillich
states that both question and answer "lie within the
'theological circle.'" Or as he states it elsewhere:
"Theology formulates the questions implied in human
existence, and theology formulates the answers
implied in the divine self-manifestation under the

guidance of the questions implied in human existence."[89] In the light of our analysis, the Method is misunderstood if the actual formulation of the questions is seen to be a philosophic task.[90] A careful reading of those sections where Tillich summarizes the five parts of his system will sustain our assertion.[91] Philosophy does not discover the existential questions and formulate them as such; instead, it gives an analysis of "man's essential nature" and of "man's existential self-estrangement" (etc.). Philosophy's task is to lay bare, clearly and decisively, the human situation. The questions are found to be "implied" in the analysis. Seeking to interpret Tillich as consistently as possible we conclude that the theologian looks at the human situation as analyzed philosophically and then he formulates, as a theologian, the specific existential questions which will correlate with the Christian message.[92] Thus while the description of the human situation is a philosophic task, the formulated questions as well as the answers are found to be within the "theological ellipse"--raised and answered by the theologian as theologian. As an apologetic theologian, then, Tillich hopes to show that the questions do reflect our human situation and that the Christian message does carry a healing answer.

We must now turn to a consideration of the role of reason in the second aspect of the Method-- that of the elaboration of the Christian answers. What place does reason have in the answers of "revelation," "God," "the Christ," "the Spirit," and "the Kingdom of God"? Tillich intends no ambiguity at this point. These saving answers are in no way to be derived from the creativity of human reason as such; rather these answers are "graced" answers which are spoken to man in his situation.

The existential question, namely, man himself in the conflicts of his existential situation, is not the source for the revelatory answers formulated by theology. One cannot derive the divine self-manifestation from an analysis of

151

the human predicament.[93]

Tillich uses more traditional terminology in other
citations:

> Paul makes it very clear what he thinks is the
> foundation of all theology: the Divine Spirit.
> And the word of wisdom and knowledge, theology,
> according to the witness of the whole Christian
> Church, is basically a gift of the Spirit. . . .
> The word of knowledge--theology--is spoken to
> us before we can say it to others, or even to
> ourselves.[94]

> In terms of classical theology one could say
> that no one can receive revelation /and thus
> the saving answer/ except through the divine
> Spirit and that, if someone is grasped by the
> Divine Spirit, the center of his personality
> is transformed; he has received saving power.[95]

Certainly Tillich is expressing, here, a primary
Christian theme--that any saving work is always
God's work, not man's. The answers to man's
dilemma is God's answer which is not discovered by
man, but revealed to him.

If the answers, then, are revealed, what is
the nature of this "revelation?" To begin with,
Tillich would set aside as a "distortion" the
"popularly understood" concept of revelation as
"divine information about matters, given to
prophets and apostles and dictated by the divine
Spirit to the writers of the Bible, or the Koran,
or other sacred books."[96] Revelation is not to be
seen as new information about the Divine or a set
of propositions which must be accepted by the faithful. It should be understood as a manifestation to
and through experience which transforms the general
perspective of him who receives the revelation and
puts life and its meaning in a new light. Specifically, Tillich defines revelation as a "special
and extraordinary manifestation which removes the
veil from something which is hidden in a special

152

and extraordinary way."[97] From a slightly different
perspective he writes: "Revelation is the manifestation of what concerns us ultimately."[98] Perhaps
his most comprehensive definition is phrased in
another work:

> Revelation is first of all the experience in
> which an ultimate concern grasps the human mind
> and creates a community in which this concern
> expresses itself in symbols of action, imagin-
> ation and thought. . . . It is an event in
> which the ultimate becomes manifest in an
> ultimate concern, shaking and transforming the
> given situation in religion and culture.[99]

The accent is on "experience" rather than cognitive
knowledge.

> Revelation of that which is essentially and
> necessarily mysterious means the manifestation
> of something within the context of ordinary
> experience which transcends the ordinary context
> of experience. Something more is known of the
> mystery after it has become manifest in
> revelation. First, its reality has become a
> matter of experience. Second, our relation to
> it has become a matter of experience. Both of
> these are cognitive elements. But revelation
> does not dissolve the mystery into knowledge.[100]

Since revelation involves the experiential
and the relational, it is always a specific revelation
and never revelation in general. That is, "it is
always revelation for someone and for a group in a
definite environment, under unique circumstances."[101]
There is the subjective side, wherein someone is
grasped, and the objective side, which is the
occurrence through which "the mystery of revelation
grasps someone."[102] The subjective side has sometimes been called "ecstasy," while the objective
side has traditionally been called "miracle."
"Ecstasy" is not to be confused with enthusiasm or
overexcitement. Rather ecstasy ("standing outside
of one's self")

points to a state of mind which is extraordinary
in the sense that the mind transcends its
ordinary situation. Ecstasy is not a negation
of reason; it is the state of mind in which
reason is beyond itself, that is, beyond its
subject-object structure. In being beyond itself reason does not deny itself. "Ecstatic
reason' remains reason; . . ."[103]

"Miracle," on the other hand, does not "designate a
happening that contradicts the laws of nature,"
instead it designates a "sign-event" through which
some revelatory experience takes place.[104] Such
a sign-event does not contradict or destroy either
the rational structure of the mind or the rational
structure of reality. Nor does "miracle" imply
that some supernatural element has interfered with
the natural processes. If the manifestation of the
ground of being through miracle necessitated the
negation of the structure of being then a "religious
dualism" would be asserted. A "genuine miracle"
must be an event which is "astonishing" and "shaking" (without contradicting the structure of
reality); it must be an event which "points to the
mystery of being" and which expresses its relation
to us in a definite way; and it must be an
occurrence which is received by someone as a "sign-
event in an ecstatic experience."[105] Miracles are
truly "miracles" only for those who receive them
as such, as sign-events.

        Those aspects of reality through which
mystery is revealed are called "mediums" of revelation.[106] Nature is one such medium. While no thing
or person is worthy in itself to represent our
ultimate concern, nevertheless there is "no reality,
thing, or event which cannot become a bearer of
the mystery of being and enter into a revelatory
correlation." In this sense, the finite can contain
the infinite since the finite "participates in
being-itself, that is, in the ground and meaning
of being." Revelation can also come through history
in that groups and personalities "can become mediums
of revelation in connection with historical events
of a revelatory character."[107] In this way the

154

people of Israel who had an ecstatic experience in relation to their historical destiny became a medium of revelation for other groups. So, also the Church is "the bearer of revelation for nations and individuals." Persons, too, can become such mediums. Indeed sainthood should be understood not as a condition of moral or spiritual perfection, but as that state wherein someone "become transparent to the ground of being."

Man is characterized by his expression of reason in language; hence, revelation cannot be "understood without the word as a medium of revelation."[108] But revelation through words must <u>not</u> be understood as an equivalent of "revealed words." Revelation involves ordinary language in that ordinary language "is made a vehicle for expressing and denoting the extraordinary experience of mind and reality in ecstasy and sign-event."[109] While words ordinarily denote general meanings and express attitudes, words used in the situation of revelation point beyond the usual denotations and expressions to the "unexpress ible and its relation to us." Words, it seems, like saints, become "transparent" to the ground of being.

Revelation also mediates knowledge, but it is a knowledge that can be "known" only in a "revelatory situation, through ecstasy and miracle."[110] The knowing must be linked to the situation, it cannot be abstracted from a situation and passed on as information. This knowledge of revelation is not "information about the nature of beings and their relation to one another," nor is it new information about the structures of nature, history, and man. It is a "knowledge about the revelation of the mystery of being to us." Revelation does not offer objective facts, but it speaks about our relation to God. The knowledge of revelation does not and should not interfere with ordinary knowledge which is guided by its own criteria of validity. Theologians, therefore, should not prefer one scientific view to another, or one psychological doctrine to another on the basis of a theological stance. (This mistake has had its part in the history of the so-called warfare of science with religion.)

155

The truth of revelation must be judged from within the dimensions of revelatory knowledge; this implies that a doctrine of final revelation must be made explicit so that revelation can be judged by its own implicit criteria. Here, too, the theologian must stand within a "circle." "Christianity claims to be based on the revelation in Jesus as the Christ as the final revelation."[111] "Final," here, does not mean "last" in a chronological sense, but it means "the decisive, fulfilling, unsurpassable revelation, that which is the criterion of all the others. This is the Christian claim, and this is the basis of a Christian theology."[112] The theologian who thinks within the church, claims, with the church, Peter's faith judgment: "Thou art the Christ" (Mw. 16:16). Two main characteristics of Jesus as the Christ are reflected in the New Testament witness: "his maintenance of unity with God and his sacrifice of everything he could have gained for himself through this unity."[113] Because of his unity with God, Jesus as the Christ becomes "transparent" to the divine mystery. It is not his moral, intellectual, or emotional quality that makes him the Christ, but the presence of God in him. His "works, deeds, and sufferings are consequences of this presence." His being is an expression of "New Being," the "New Creation" in which the Christian participates.[114] But Jesus as the Christ is not to be understood as an end himself; rather, he is transparent to the divine. Jesus' total sacrifice of himself, through his acceptance of the cross, permits total transparency since such a sacrifice vitiates any attempt to make Jesus of Nazareth into an idol and allows Jesus as the Christ to point to Him who is greater (John 14:28). To be sure, Jesus is the Christ only for those who accept him as such, and this acceptance itself is an aspect of the revelatory event, a work of the divine Spirit.[115] Faith is always a gift.

Any consideration of the relation between reason and the answers supplied by the Christian message must take special notice of the link which Tillich makes between revelation and salvation.[116]

"Revelation can be received only in the presence
of salvation, and salvation can occur only within a
correlation of revelation." To participate ecstati-
cally in a revelatory event means to become transformed through that event, as Paul learned on the
road to Damascus--though Paul had no new "information" because of the event. Both revelation and
salvation are works of divine grace. "In terms of
classical theology one could say that no one can
receive revelation except through the divine Spirit
and that, if someone is grasped by the divine
Spirit, the center of his personality is transformed;
he has received saving power."[117] Such salvation
and revelation are always fragmentary under the
conditions of existence with respect to the persons
who "receive revelatory truth and saving power."
Ultimate salvation and ultimate revelation, with
regard to the receiving persons, is often spoken of
in terms of the "vision of God." Reflecting his
vision of the unity of reality, Tillich understands
this ultimate fulfillment of the "vision of God"
as universal, not individual. Indeed, no individual
could be meaningfully fulfilled "apart from the
salvation of everyone and everything."

Final revelation heals the whole man. In
such a healing event final revelation overcomes
"the conflicts of reason in existence."[118] Autonomy and heteronomy are overcome in a theonomous
union. That which had been seen as over-against
the autonomous self is now seen as the depth of
the self. The divine law is understood to be an
essential expression of the self. Absolutism and
relativism are overcome by the final revelation
manifest in Jesus as the Christ. In this personal
life the Christian faith claims universal and
unconditional validity; yet this same life cannot
be used as a source for absolute ethics, doctrines,
or ideals. Jesus as the Christ points to the
absolute, he is not the absolute himself. Finally,
the conflict between formalism and emotionalism
is overcome.[119] Participating knowledge (the
emotional aspect) is not in conflict with technical

(formalized) knowledge since both are grounded in the same Logos. This "Alexandrian" solution is the only way of overcoming this conflict.

Our concern here has been to illustrate Tillich's point of view, not to present a detailed analysis or critique of this "healing" of reason. In summary, there is no conflict between reason and faith; and revelation does not set reason aside or destroy reason, it fulfills it.

Ecstasy is fulfilled, not denied, rationality. Reason can be fulfilled only if it is driven beyond the limits of its finitude, and experiences the presence of the ultimate, the holy. Without such an experience reason exhausts itself and its finite contents and is destroyed by them. The road leads from reason fulfilled in faith through reason without faith to reason filled with demonic-destructive faith. The second stage is only a stage of transition. . .[120]

Since he stands within the theological "circle" of a faith commitment, the theologian apparently would claim that his reason is fulfilled, at least fragmentarily. How, then, is this healed reason related to the elaboration of the content of the Christian message? Tillich maintains that two forms of cognition are involved for the theologian.[121] One form of cognition pertains to the technical, scholarly work of the theologian and can best be seen as an aspect of "technical" or formal reason (as the study of the history of Christian thought, and the critical study of scripture). The theologian shares this type of cognition with all those who take part in scholarly endeavors. There is, however, a second kind of cognition "implied in faith which is qualitatively different" from this first form. The organ for the reception of this second kind of cognition is labeled "self-transcending" or "ecstatic" reason. This ecstatic reason is reason that has been grasped by an ultimate concern, and is "overpowered, invaded, and shaken" by this ultimate concern. As a technical scholar the theologian works over and systematizes the contents

of the Christian faith as it is developed from the
various sources. As a man in faith, however, the
theologian finds that the "contents of the faith
grasp" his reason. As a believer the theologian
participates in the truth of the faith, as a
scholar he investigates faith's contents. It appears
that Tillich does not hold that the Christian theologian, as a man of Christian faith, knows more
about the Christian faith than does a scholar outside the faith stance. The difference is to be
found in the man's relation to the contents of the
faith. As a scholar a man can be detached from
the contents; as believer the theologian is claimed
by the contents. This is only to reassert the view
that revelation is not new knowledge or information,
but a new condition.

The contents of the Christian faith, which
the theologian as scholar and believer develops,
is not to be produced, as such, from either technical or ecstatic reason. Reason is not a source
for the theologian, but a type of instrument which
works with the sources and thus develops the
contents.[122] Tillich elaborates the sources for
systematic theology in the introduction to his major
work. The three sources which he discusses possess
varying "degrees of importance . . . corresponding
with /their/ more direct or more indirect relationship to the central event on which the Christian
faith is based, the appearance of the New Being in
Jesus as the Christ."[123] The implication is clear
that the sources focus on the event of final revelation which shaped the first Christian community
and which has, therefore, fed the streams of Christian
history. As the "original document about the events
on which Christianity is based," the Bible is the
basic source of systematic theology.[124] The
"inspiration" of the Biblical writers consists of
their acceptance of Jesus as the Christ. These
writers are part of the original event insofar as
they were involved in the act of reception which
is always an aspect of revelation. Thus the Bible
is part of the original event and witnesses to the
original event.

A second source for systematic theology is church history.[125] The Bible as source implies church history as source since the "genesis of the Bible is an event in church history." Furthermore, every contemporary Christian is guided in his understanding of the Bible by the generations of Christians who have preceded him. No one can leap over two thousand years of history and become contemporaneous with the Biblical writers. The theologian accepts this history as his history, and he seeks to include a critical and an existentially concerned element in his use of the Bible and the history of Christian thought. The third, and broadest, source for systematic theology is the material presented by "the history of religion and culture."[126] Since the theologian is inevitably involved as a person in his cultural context (e.g., his use of language itself), he should recognize the part this cultural setting plays in his thought. This source is especially related to the "question" side of the Method, since it is the analysis of man's culture and concerns which prepares the way for an answering theology.

The three sources, as outlined, can be considered as sources only for someone who "participates in them." Therefore, a theologian must consider the place of experience which is the means of such participation.[127] Schleiermacher's experiential method cannot be ignored, whether or not one agrees or disagrees with it. The role of experience is central, but Schleiermacher erred by seeking to derive the contents of the Christian faith _from_ what he called the "Religious consciousness" of the Christian. Tillich sees experience as a medium, not a source.

The event on which Christianity is based . . . is not derived from experience; it is _given_ in history. Experience is not the source from which the contents of systematic theology are taken but the medium through which they are existentially received.[128]

Given the almost endless amount of material that can come from the sources through experience, a

theological norm must be established as a guide
for any systematic work.[129] Both material norms
(a creed for Catholicism, and "justification through
faith" for Protestantism) and formal norms (the
hierarchy for Roman Catholicism, and the Bible for
Protestantism) have appeared in Christian history.
The Protestant material norm reflects the spiritual
setting in which Protestantism developed; furthermore, there are other analogous norms which have
developed in the history of the church (e.g., the
"liberation of finite man from death and error by
the incarnation of immortal life and truth" was a
norm for the early Greek church). Thus norms develop
within history by way of a process that is largely
unconscious, though many conscious decisions are
involved. "The norm grows; it is not produced intentionally; its appearance is not the work of theological reflection but of the Spiritual life of the
church, for the church is the 'home' of systematic
theology."[130] Tillich presents his norm, to be
used as a criterion in his system, with "reservations" since a genuine norm is not the private
opinion of a theologian, but an expression of an
encounter of the church itself with the Christian
message. Thus history must eventually become the
judge of the norm which he selects.

The norm itself is directly related to the
correlating process, for an analysis of contemporary man will describe the situation to which the
norm must relate. The question arising out of man's
experience today is not that of a merciful God (as
in the Reformation) or the question of finitude (as
in the early Greek Church); rather it is a "question
of a reality in which the self-estrangement of our
existence is overcome, a reality of reconciliation
and reunion, of creativity, meaning and hope."[131]
Such a reality Tillich calls the "New Being," a
term based on Paul's message of the "new creation"
(II Cor. 5:17; Gal. 6:15). As the message of the
New Being, Christianity provides the answers for the
questions "implied in our present situation and in
every human situation." The New Being is manifest
in "Jesus as the Christ"--an assertion which accepts
the ancient Christian confession as central. Thus

161

Tillich states his material norm as the "New Being in Jesus as the Christ as our ultimate concern. This norm is the criterion for the use of all the sources of systematic theology."[132] The Bible, as a collection of religious literature that is not particularly homogeneous, stands under the norm and is interpreted in the light of the norm. Yet in another sense the Bible shapes the norm itself since the norm is derived from an "encounter of the church with the biblical message."

The integrity of Tillich's system is maintained in the norm which he selects, for this norm, with its derivation, reflects not only his method of correlation but also the basically Christocentric nature of his theology. Furthermore, his analysis of the developmental process which produces the norm reflects nicely his "organismic" view of historical, spiritual, and personal life. One gains a sense of a living church participating in a living history grounded in a "living" God--to speak, of course, symbolically.[133] In this living history the spiritual life of man, with its own dynamics, is developed and expressed. The Method seeks to keep in touch with the dynamic aspects of life and history while remaining grounded in that truth of "final revelation" which was manifest in the Christ event.

In closing our discussion of the nature and the role of reason in Tillich's theological enterprise, we should consider specifically the area of man's knowledge of God. As our analysis above shows, the "answers" of theology are given to man, they are not derived from man himself as he reflects on the nature of life and the world. It is not surprising, therefore, to find that Tillich denies the possibility of "natural theology"--if such a term would mean that, "without existential participation in an ultimate concern, a detached analysis of reality can produce theological propositions."[134] Such an assertion leans back upon other facets of his thinking; i.e.: 1) a theologian deals, by definition, with ultimate concern; thus a detached attitude is impossible in anything "theological"; 2) a

162

theologian does not "choose" but is "chosen by" an ultimate concern--he is "grasped"--; thus theological propositions do not stem from a line of logical arguments and inferences, but are elaborations which grow out of revelatory events.

In denying the possibility of a "natural theology" Tillich would, of course, set himself against any of the so-called arguments for the existence of God.[135] These arguments fail since both the "concept of existence and the method of arguing to a conclusion are inadequate for the idea of God." God is not a being among other beings. "God does not exist. He is being-itself beyond essence and existence. Therefore, to argue that God exists is to deny him."[136] To argue from the world of experience or thought to the conclusion "God" also contradicts the idea of God; for to derive God from the world (not in the sense that he is dependent on the world) implies that he "cannot be that which transcends the world infinitely." Such arguments are really only attempts to make "God" into a "missing link" that will answer such questions as "Where from?" and "How?" and "Toward what end?"

To explain why so many leading theologians have been almost equally divided over the validity of these "arguments," Tillich asserts that one group did not attack what the other group, in fact, defended. "Those who attacked the arguments for the existence of God criticized their argumentative form; those who defended them accepted their implicit meaning."[137] If the arguments are failures as arguments, Tillich feels that such arguments are an expression of a truth.

They are expressions of the question of God which is implied in human finitude. This question is their truth; every answer they give is untrue. . . . The question of God is possible because an awareness of God is present in the question of God. This awareness precedes the question. It is not the result of the argument but its presupposition.[138]

163

Thus the so-called ontological argument is not so much an argument as it is a reflection of "an awareness of the infinite" which is included in "man's awareness of finitude." In his awareness of his finitude, man is aware of an infinity which belongs to him though he is excluded from it. The ontological argument, then, is to be seen as an implied analysis of man's finitude and the questions which are themselves implied in such finitude. Insofar as it is analysis and not argument it is valid.[139]

Within finitude, then, man experiences an element which transcends finitude as such. Augustine, Kant, and Plato in their ways have elaborated positions which reflect this element as the presence of something "unconditional within the self and the world."[140] This unconditional element appears as the true-itself (verum ipsum) which is the norm for all truth; as the good-itself (bonum ipsum) which is the norm for all goodness; and being-itself (esse ipsum) which is the "ground and abyss of everything that is."[141] These various expressions of the unconditional element in experience are valid as analytical descriptions of the structure of reality, but they establish neither the reality of God, nor any specific content of truth or goodness. This unconditional element appears as part of the philosophic analysis of man and his experience, and thus becomes part of the material out of which the theologian formulates the existential questions. To identify this unconditional element with the reality of God, as Augustine did when he identified verum ipsum with the God of the church, is to move out of the realm of philosophical analysis and into the realm of theological assertions.[142] Augustine's identification is a judgment of faith; but the immediate awareness of an unconditional element is self-evident and not a matter of faith. Faith moves beyond this element since faith always involves a risk. "The risk of faith is based on the fact that the unconditional element can become a matter of ultimate concern only if it appears in a concrete embodiment."[143] In other words, we tend to choose (or are chosen by) certain concrete aspects of reality as criteria for the specific content of the uncon-

ditional element--since to live with seriousness is
to decide what is "true" or "good." The concrete
choice we make may, in fact, be at least partially
in error, if not wholly; thus we risk the meaning
and fulfilment of our lives. Yet choose we must,
even though the element of doubt persists. Still
the "profoundest doubt could not undermine the
presupposition of doubt, the awareness of something
unconditional."[144]

It is clear, then, that Tillich intends to
dismiss anything that would come under the traditional label of "natural theology." Yet he feels that
the persistent interest in such reflects an "unconditional element" in human experience out of which
the question of God can be formulated. However,
let us recall that the actual formulation of such
a question is a theological task which takes place
within the theological ellipse. The question of
God "is possible only because the transcendental
has already dragged us out beyond ourselves as we
have received answers which drive us to the quest."[145]
It would seem to be consistent, then, to conclude
that any exposition of the nature of God is a theological, not a philosophical, exposition which is
grounded in the sources and norm of systematic
theology. Ontology may elaborate the structure of
being, but the identification of "being-itself"
with God is, we have established, a theological
assertion.

> The ontological structure of being supplies
> the material for the symbols which point to the
> divine life. However, this does not mean that
> a doctrine of God can be derived from an
> ontological system. The character of the divine
> life is made manifest in revelation. Theol-
> ogy can only explain and systematize the exis-
> tential knowledge of revelation in theoretical
> terms, interpreting the symbolic significance
> of the ontological elements and categories.[146]

This would mean that while the first section of Part
II ("Being and God") is a philosophical analysis that
lays the groundwork for the question of God, the

second section which explicates the "Reality of God"
is fully theological in that the assertions, while
correlated with the ontological analysis, are grounded
in an accepted revelatory event, that of Jesus as the
Christ. In other words, to illustrate the idea of
"feed-back" which we have mentioned earlier, the
positive element of content in Part II is actually
dependent upon material which is contained in both
parts III and IV (Existence and the Christ; Life and
the Spirit) of Systematic Theology. Tillich puts it
this way in Part I of the system: "A doctrine of God
as the ground of revelation presupposes the doctrine
of Being and God, which, on the other hand, is dependent
on the doctrine of revelation."[147] And in Part II
he indicates this necessary interrelationship while
dealing with the specific concept of divine love.

> The divine love is the final answer to the
> questions implied in human existence, including
> finitude, the threat of disruption, and estrange-
> ment. Actually, this answer is given only in
> the manifestation of the divine love under the
> conditions of existence. It is the christo-
> logical answer to which the doctrine of the
> divine love gives the systematic foundation,
> although one would not be able to speak of this
> foundation without having received the christo-
> logical answer. But what is existentially first,
> may be systematically last and vice versa.[148]

To cast this discussion in Luther's terms,
it seems that we cannot accuse Tillich of developing
a "theology of glory." If "the characteristics of
God are given only in revelation," then the Christian
knows God only as God gives himself to man. What
Tillich seeks to elaborate is not so much what God
is in His essence, but what He is relationally--
what he is "for us." Tillich's most explicit statements in this regard come in response to a series of
questions:

> I try, not always successfully, to avoid state-
> ments about the divine nature which transcend
> the merely relational, the "for us." . . . I

would shy away from the task of finding a
definite "structure" in God. Symbols, derived from particular experiences of the
relation to God, do not constitute a structure.
. . . .
The validity of the experience of faith (the
state of being grasped by the spiritual Presence)
is not diminished by the fact that our knowledge
of the divine ground of our being refers to its
relation to us, but not to its essence. The
mystery of being itself is beyond the cognitive
grasp of any finite being. . . . The problem
is not to find a more or less trustworthy cognitive approach to the divine, either by faith
or by "the reasonable probability" of inference;
the problem is one of participation itself.[149]

We think that Tillich is largely consistent with this
expressed intent. A survey of his considerations of
the "Reality of God" in Part II indicates that the
accent is on the relational aspect of the divine-
human encounter, not on the essential nature of God
as He is in Himself.

        As a closing observation we note that A. T.
Mollegen has written that Tillich's theology is
"radically Christocentric."[150] Our analysis of
Tillich's Method would lead us to concur. Certainly
his choice of the material norm (the New Being in
Jesus as the Christ as our ultimate concern) is
anchored in this Christological focus and thus
controls, in intent, the entire substance of the
theological project. Furthermore, the genuinely
saving (or "healing") aspects of Christian faith are
centered in the Christ event. This accent is reflected
in the second volume of Systematic Theology, for here
we get an analysis of man as he finds himself in the
conditions of existence. Here is the picture of man
in his need, in his estrangement, in his brokenness--
man as he finds himself apart from the saving Word.
And it is here where we find the description of the
New Being in Jesus as the Christ who brings and is
the saving reality. Here is where the "final revelation" is set forth--that revelation which is to be

167

identified with salvation. As Tillich once stated the matter: "For we are real theologians when we state that Jesus is the Christ, and that it is in Him that the Logos of theology is manifest."[151]

FOOTNOTES

1. Tillich, Biblical Religion and . . . , p. 85.
2. S.T., I, 71.
3. S.T., I, 71. Tillich cites those periods
which produced ancient skepticism, Descartes, Hume,
and Kant as examples of such a shift in focus. For
instance, Plato's epistemology grows out of his
ontology, while Descartes' ontology must await his
epistemological solution.
4. S.T., I, 71.
5. See S.T., I, 57-59.
6. See S.T., I, 72 ff., for much of the following
material. There are interesting similarities, here,
to Augustine's distinction between "wisdom" and
"science." Cf. J.V.L. Casserly, The Christian in
Philosophy (New York: Charles Scribner's Sons, 1955),
p. 46.
7. S.T., I, 72.
8. Tillich, Dynamics of Faith, p. 75.
9. S.T., I, 72-73.
10. The American pragmatist philosophers thoroughly reflect this technical use of reason.
11. S.T., I, 73.
12. Paul Tillich, The Shaking of the Foundations
(New York: Charles Scribner's Sons, 1948), p. 62.
13. S.T., I, 75.
14. S.T., I, 76. By "reality" Tillich seems to
mean, in this context, the whole of the phenomenological world which confronts us in our existence.
This world which we experience is the reality we can
understand through our rational nature. Tillich's
writings abound in metaphor. While he insists that
he seeks semantic clarity, one of the common criticisms
of his work is the nebulous nature of his language.
See J. H. Thomas, Paul Tillich: An Appraisal (Philadelphia: Westminster Press, 1963), for a work which
criticizes Tillich extensively on the basis of
ambiguous and fuzzy language. James Luther Adams,
in his Paul Tillich's Philosophy of Culture, Science,
and Religion (New York: Harper and Row, 1965), pp.
1-16, suggests that Tillich's search for a new and
more effective language is at least in part responsible for the semantic flavor of his writings.

Certainly Tillich sees nothing sacrosanct in traditional religious terminology as such.

15. <u>S.T.</u>, I, 77.

16. <u>S.T.</u>, I, 77-78. Tillich suggests that there
are four classical ways in which the relationship
between subjective and objective reason has been
seen. 1) Realism--which "considers subjective reason
as an effect of the whole of reality on a part of it,
namely, on the mind." 2) Idealism--which "considers
objective reason as a creation of subjective reason
on the basis of an unstructured matter in which it
actualizes itself." 3) Dualism (or pluralism)--
which affirms the "ontological independence and the
functional interdependence of subjective and objective
reason." 4) Monism--"which affirms an underlying
identity which expresses itself in the rational
structure of reality." (<u>S.T.</u>, I, 75-76).

17. <u>S.T.</u>, I, 79.

18. <u>S.T.</u>, I, 79.

19. The mood and language of Tillich's thought
at this point has a distinct family resemblance to
the so-called argument for the existence of God
from first cause or from contingency. We shall see
later that Tillich denies the validity of such
arguments.

20. <u>S.T.</u>, I, 81.

21. Tillich, <u>Biblical Religion and</u> . . ., p.55.

22. <u>S.T.</u>, I, 81. The interdependence of the
various parts of the <u>Systematic Theology</u> is clearly
discernible in this section, for he elaborates the
dilemma of actual reason in terms of elements
explored more fully in parts II, III, and IV.

23. <u>S.T.</u>, I, 83.

24. <u>S.T.</u>, I, 83.

25. See <u>S.T.</u>, I, 83-94, for an elaboration of
these conflicts. This "emotional" element seems to
be a blood relative of Nietzsche's "Dionysian" model.
Cf. Walter Kaufman, <u>From Shakespeare to Existentialism</u>
(Anchor Books; Garden City: Doubleday and Co., Inc.,
1960), pp. 229-230, 292 ff.

26. <u>S.T.</u>, I, 94.

27. Tillich, <u>Biblical Religion and</u> . . .,pp.8-9.

28. <u>Ibid.</u>, p. 13.

29. <u>Ibid.</u>, p. 10.

30. _Ibid._, p. vii. On p. 75 Tillich points out that the theological concept of an incarnate _logos_ is deeply dependent upon a philosophical tradition.

31. Paul Tillich, "Relation of Metaphysics and Theology," _Review of Metaphysics_, Vol. X (September, 1956), p. 61.

32. S.T., I, 22.

33. S.T., I, 22.

34. S.T., I, 23. In another context Tillich asserts that these contrasting attitudes are largely overcome in the man who is the philosopher or theologian. Both philosopher and theologian, as men, carry the same risks; the risk of the adequacy of their ultimate concern, the "risk about the meaning of one's being." Thus in the man, if not in the formal disciplines, the distinction in attitude is overcome. This leaves both the theologian and philosopher open to the possibility of fanaticism. Cf. "Relation of Metaphysics . . . ," p. 62.

35. S.T., I, 23-24.

36. S.T., I, 24.

37. S.T., I, 24-28.

38. S.T., I, 25. Cf. Tillich's observation in his "Relation of Metaphysics . . . ," p. 59: "No philosophy is without an ultimate concern in its background, whether this is acknowledged or denied. This makes the philosopher a theologian, always implicitly and sometimes explicitly." Cf. also Tillich's comment in Sydney and Beatrice Rome, _Philosophical Interrogations_ (New York: Holt, Rinehart and Winston, 1964), p. 373; "My concept of a philosopher is that he is first of all a human being who is rooted in one of the great cultural and religious traditions which originate in revelatory experiences and their mythical expressions. . . . he cannot liberate himself from the substance of his tradition. . . . Plato remains always a 'son of Apollo' and Spinoza a 'successor of Amos.'"

39. There are, of course, those who bristle at Tillich's terminology since they have no desire to be associated either with "religion" or "theology." However, Tillich has no desire to baptize anyone into a tradition through linguistic manipulation. If his definitions are seen as the formal definitions that they are, the terms carry no "believing"

171

connotation; though it seems fair to say that Tillich gives these terms a content which varies from common usage. Since there seems to be no final definition of what "religion" (or "Theology" for that matter) is, Tillich has chosen to suggest one that he feels is helpful in exploring and articulating the phenomenon and experience of religion in general and Christianity in particular.

40. <u>S.T.</u>, I, 25.
41. <u>S.T.</u>, I, 26.
42. <u>S.T.</u>, I, 26.
43. <u>S.T.</u>, I, 26.
44. The failure to understand Tillich's distinction between philosophy and theology is reflected by certain philosophers (and theologians) who criticize him. Cf. Marvin Fox, "Tillich's Ontology and God," <u>Angelican Theological Review</u>, Vol. XLIII (July, 1961), pp. 260-267. Fox is offended by Tillich's assertion (surely a theological, not a philosophical assertion) that the Christian revelation is somehow final; and he suggests that Tillich should offer some kind of conclusive <u>reasons</u> why such a Christian claim may be made. Fox thereby calls Tillich to be a full-blown "natural theologian," a task Tillich would label as self-contradictory.

45. <u>S.T.</u>, I, 28.
46. Bernard Martin, <u>The Existentialist Theology of Paul Tillich</u> (New York: Bookman Associates, 1963), p. 19.
47. <u>Ibid.</u>, p. 27. For a helpful, though brief, description of Husserl's method as it relates to various existentialist thinkers, see Cobb, <u>op. cit.</u>, chapter 8. Tillich has a brief description of the phenomenological method in <u>S.T.</u>, I, 106 ff., where he shows that while this method is applicable to the realm of "logical meanings" it is "only partially competent in the realm of spiritual realities."
48. Martin, <u>op. cit.</u>, p. 27; Cobb, <u>op. cit.</u>, p. 262.
49. <u>S.T.</u>, I, 23.
50. See Cobb, <u>op. cit.</u>, pp. 263 ff., for a very helpful discussion of this material. Tillich's <u>Dynamics of Faith</u> is a well developed presentation of his analysis of the meaning of faith. Another interesting use of phenomenological analysis is to be

found in Tillich's description of "revelation." His
intent is to present a description which would cover
"all possible and actual revelations" (S.T., I, 132).
Yet he points out that the primary example of revelation, which is chosen as a norm, is chosen on the
basis of a faith judgment--that, in fact, such an
example is considered to be final. He calls this
approach "critical phenomenology" which unites "an
intuitive-descriptive element with an existential-
critical element." (S.T., I, 107.)

    51. Cobb, op. cit., p. 265.
    52. Ibid., p. 268; S.T., I, 164.
    53. S.T., I, 169.
    54. S.T., I, 173.
    55. See S.T., I, 164 ff., for a detailed develop-
ment.

    56. Recall that Tillich insists ontology is
philosopher's work, although a theologian needs to
be familiar with the field. See S.T., I, 164.

    57. S.T., I, 168.
    58. S.T., I, 168-169. Tillich cites Heidegger's
work in Sein und Zeit as an application of this
insight.

    59. Cf. Martin, op. cit., p. 82.
    60. S.T., I, 176.
    61. S.T., I, 176. See, also, S.T., I, 260-261.
Here Tillich grants that these concepts of "participation" and "microcosmos" are hard to understand in
"a culture which is determined by nominalism and
individuals."

    62. Paul Tillich, Theology of Culture (Galaxy
Books; New York: Oxford University Press, 1964),
p. 46. We can safely infer that Tillich refers
expecially to various expressions of existentialism
when he speaks, here, of philosophy.

    63. Ibid., p. 117.
    64. Paul Tillich, "The Impact of Pastoral
Psychology on Theological Thought," The Ministry and
Mental Health, ed. Hans Hofmann (New York: Association
Press, 1960), p. 14. Throughout this article Tillich
shows how a field such as psychology can be very
helpful in describing man's dilemma.

    65. S.T., II, 15.
    66. McKelway, op. cit., p. 69.
    67. Johnson, op. cit., p. 119.

68. Harvey Cox, The Secular City (Macmillan paperback; New York: The Macmillan Co., 1965), pp. 79-81. Cox asserts: "In the age of the secular city, the questions with which we concern ourselves tend to be mostly functional and operational. We ask. . . pragmatic questions, and we are pragmatic men whose interest in religion is at best peripheral." Yet in the same breath, Cox, asserts: "It is true that at the center of our pragmatic questions we can hear echoes of older ones about how to be saved, how to overcome guilt and insufficiency, how to dissern significance, and how to live purposefully." Cox does not quite want to let go of these "ultimate questions." On the other hand, Tillich considers any attempt to repress the question of meaning as a "neurotic way out" (Theology of Culture, p. 46).
69. Tillich, Theology of Culture, pp. 202 ff.
70. Tillich, Biblical Religion and . . . , p. 14.
71. S.T., II, 13.
72. Tillich, Theology of Culture, pp. 204-205.
73. Ibid., pp. 205-206. Underlining is mine.
74. Ibid., p. 154.
75. Ibid., p. 42. Underlining mine. For an autobiographical account of how Tillich understands the impact of cultural experience on a person's religious make-up, see his Interpretation of History, pp. 41 ff., where he describes his own background as one living "on the Boundary Between Church and Society."
76. S.T., I, 27.
77. Tillich, "What is Wrong . . . ," p. 137. See his The Shaking of . . . , pp. 128-129, where Tillich analyzes Paul's "Mar's Hill Sermon" in the light of this approach.
78. Tillich, "The Problem of . . . ,"p. 280.
79. S.T., I, 61.
80. S.T., II, 79.
81. S.T., I, 137.
82. S.T., I, 139.
83. S.T., I, 146.
84. Tillich, The Shaking of . . . , p. 139.
85. From a sermon entitled, "Heal the Sick . . . Cast Out Demons," included in Tillich's A History of Christian Thought, p. 271.
86. S.T., I, 61.

87. Rome, op. cit., p. 372.
88. Cf. the following from Theology of Culture, p. 208; "Our answers must have as many forms as there are questions and situations, individual and social . . . . In former centuries of Christian history, the authorities formulated as the biblical message, often unconsciously, those points which gave answers to the temporal and spatial situation of their people, including themselves. They formulated as the biblical message that which could be communicated to themselves as well as to the masses."
89. S.T., I, 61.
90. Cf. S.T., II, 13-14. Robert Johnson, op. cit., pp. 112 ff., wrestles mightily with this problem of interpretation.
91. See S.T., I, 66-67; and Tillich, "The Problem of . . . ," pp. 279-280.
92. Cf. S.T., II, 14-15; and S.T., I, 63. If the question-answer interrelation is understood to be within the "theological circle" (or "ellipse"), then McKelway's and Johnson's criticisms from a Barthian point of view are substantially undercut (See footnotes 66 and 67 in this chapter). The "questions" are not only "man's" questions, but "Christian" questions since they are formulated within the framework of a Christian faith stance. "The material of the existential question is taken from the whole of human experience and its manifold ways of expression. . . . The choice of the material, as well as the formulation of the question, is the task of the systematic theologian."(S.T., II, 15. Underlining mine.)
93. S.T., II, 13.
94. Tillich, The Shaking of . . . , p. 119.
95. S.T., I, 146.
96. Tillich, Dynamics of Faith, p. 78.
97. S.T., I, 108.
98. S.T., I, 110.
99. Tillich, Dynamics of Faith, pp. 78-79.
100. S.T., I, 109. Underlining mine.
101. Tillich, Biblical Religion and . . . , p. 3.
102. S.T., I, 111.
103. S.T., I, 111-112. An attempt to interpret these metaphors would, I fear, only involve my own metaphors. So I let Tillich speak for himself.

104. <u>S.T.</u>, I, 115 ff.
105. <u>S.T.</u>, I, 117.
106. <u>S.T.</u>, I, 118 ff. In his phenomenological account of revelation, Tillich seeks to show why various phenomena of nature such as heavenly bodies, seasonal changes, birth, death, sex, etc., have become important symbols in various religious traditions.
107. <u>S.T.</u>, I, 121.
108. <u>S.T.</u>, I, 122.
109. <u>S.T.</u>, I, 123.
110. <u>S.T.</u>, I, 129 ff.
111. <u>S.T.</u>, I, 132 ff.
112. Tillich goes on to show that this claim of final revelation can be justified by showing that "there are criteria within the revelation in Jesus as the Christ which make it final." But Tillich abstracts his "criteria" from that revelatory event which he has already selected as final on the grounds of a faith judgment! This totally circular approach is hardly compelling to one outside this faith stance, and is unnecessary for one who is already "grasped."
113. <u>S.T.</u>, I, 135.
114. See Paul Tillich, <u>The New Being</u> (Scribner paperback; New York: Charles Scribner's Sons, 1955), pp. 15-24, for a sermonic elaboration of the concept of "New Being." See <u>S.T.</u>, II, <u>passim</u>, for an extended development.
115. <u>S.T.</u>, I, 144.
116. See <u>S.T.</u>, I, 144-147.
117. <u>S.T.</u>, I, 146.
118. <u>S.T.</u>, I, 147.
119. <u>S.T.</u>, I, 153 ff.
120. Tillich, <u>Dynamics</u> <u>of</u> <u>Faith</u>, pp. 76-77.
121. <u>S.T.</u>, I, 53 ff.
122. The relation between reason and the sources is not a simple one, however, for the act of reception tends to have an influence on what is received. In short, Christian theology must recognize that it, too, is "subject to the contradictions of man's existential situation." (<u>S.T.</u>, I, 54).
123. <u>S.T.</u>, I, 40.
124. <u>S.T.</u>, I, 34-36. In this context Tillich asserts that theological confusion is unavoidable if the Bible is called the Word of God. Such identification has fostered a variety of unhappy consequences in

176

Christian history. The symbol "Word of God" has
as its central meaning the manifestation of God--
and this is not limited to the Bible. Tillich
develops some six different meanings of the "Word
of God," one of which is the Bible as the document
of the final revelation (S.T., I, 157-159).
    125. S.T., I, 36-38.
    126. S.T., I, 38-40.
    127. S.T., I, 40-46.
    128. S.T., I, 42.
    129. S.T., I, 47-52.
    130. S.T., I, 48.
    131. S.T., I, 49.
    132. S.T., I, 50.
    133. Certainly an intriguing, and highly
controversial, aspect of Tillich's work is his view
of the "symbolic" nature of assertions about God.
This is a notoriously difficult area of concern and
Tillich himself has had problems with the concept.
In 1951 he wrote that the statement that "God is
being-itself is a nonsymbolic statement," while all
else said about God is symbolic (S.T., I, 238-239).
While in 1957 he shifts his ground by saying that
the only "assertion about God" that is non-symbolic
is that "everything we say about God is symbolic"
(S.T., II, 9). This latter, of course, is not a
statement about God, but a statement about statements about God. Tillich seeks to tie his cluster
of symbols, somehow, to the solid ground of non-
symbolic discourse, lest he "fall into a circular
argument." For some of Tillich's discussions of
this area see: S.T., I, 238-247; S.T., II, 9-10;
"The Nature of Religious Language," Theology of
Culture, pp. 53-67; and Dynamics of Faith, pp. 41-
54. Criticisms of his stance abound. Cf. Kaufmann,
op. cit., pp. 189-196; K. Hamilton, op. cit., p. 58
et passim; J. H. Randall, "The Ontology of Paul
Tillich," Kegley and Bretall, op. cit., pp. 160-
161; Charles Hartshorne, "Tillich's Doctrine of
God," Kegley and Bretall, op. cit., pp. 182 ff.
We do not include a discussion of this topic since
what we want to describe is the basis man has for
speaking about God at all, rather than the nature
of such speaking. We wish to show that, in Tillich's
thought, man can make statements about God only on

the basis of revelation. Just _how_ language functions
in such statements is not, we feel, a critical
element in our endeavor.

134. Tillich, "The Problem of . . . ," p. 277.

135. See S.T., I, 204-210 for Tillich's discussion
of the ontological and cosmological "arguments."

136. S.T., I, 205. Tillich does feel that in
the devotional life of a Christian there is a sense
in which "God becomes a being, a person, a 'thou'
for us." But all this rests on the ground of God's
character as being itself. (Kegley and Bretall,
op. cit., p. 341.)

137. S.T., I, 204.

138. S.T., I, 205-206.

139. Tillich interprets the "cosmological arguments" in much the same way (S.T., I, 208-210).

140. S.T., I, 206. The term "unconditional"
seems to have no specific content, but it denotes
a formal element or dimension within human experience. It is that element in our experience which
impresses upon us the conviction that we stand under
and in relation to some type of structure or demand
of "truth" and "goodness," and that we are grounded
in something that transcends finitude. The unconditional is not a matter of deduction, but a "given."
It is a philosophical, not a theological concept;
the unconditional is not "God," though God is unconditioned. (Cf. Tillich, Theology of Culture, p.
24.)

141. Tillich points to Augustine's refutation
of the skeptic position and Kant's discussion of
ethical relativism as approaches which are built
upon this sense of the "unconditional." He feels,
however, that both err when they seek to argue from
this experience of an unconditional element to the
conclusion of an "unconditional being (a contradiction
in terms) within reality" (S.T., I, 207). For a
comprehensive discussion of this whole area of
"arguments" for the existence of God and the
"unconditional" element in experience see Tillich's
provocative article "The Two Types of Philosophy
of Religion," in Theology of Culture, pp. 10-29,
where he contrasts Augustine and Aquinas.

142. We should note that Tillich would consider
"being-itself" a proper philosophic term; however,
the identification of "being-itself" or the "ground

of being" with God would seem to be a theological
assertion. "The religious word for what is called
the ground of being is God" (S.T., I, 156). And
when "God" is used a multitude of denotations and
connotations, which are related to some accepted
(or rejected) final revelation, enter the scene.

143. Tillich, The Theology of Culture, p. 28.
144. Ibid., p. 29.
145. Tillich, "What is Wrong . . . ," p. 140.
146. S.T., I, 243. Underlining mine.
147. S.T., I, 156.
148. S.T., I, 286. If our analysis is right,
then John Cobb is clearly wrong in his interpretation
of Tillich's system. Cobb writes of Tillich's method:
"Thus the theologian can say nothing about God that
the ontologist has not said. . . . With respect to
what is said about God, it is ontology and not a
specific appeal to revelation in Jesus Christ that
is decisive." (Cobb, op. cit., p. 277.) Cobb
fails to distinguish between the pholosophic and
the theological side of correlation; and he fails
to see the ever-present element of "feed-back" in
the Systematic Theology in terms of the theological
content. McKelway has a much more adequate picture
of Tillich's system (op. cit., pp. 136-143). Our
implication is that one can use Luther's Law-Gospel
distinction as a helpful guide in thinking through
and interpreting Tillich's thought.

149. Rome, op. cit., pp. 378 and 388.
150. Kegley and Bretall, op. cit., p. 230.
151. Tillich, The Shaking of . . . , p. 129.

CHAPTER VI

CONCLUSIONS

In this short chapter we want to state specifically those conclusions which have been implied in the material of the last two chapters. Restating the general parallels between the Law-Gospel distinction and the method of correlation as we outlined them in Chapter III, we observe that the "existential questions" side of Tillich's method of correlation may be seen as a methodological parallel to Luther's understanding of the "theological" or "proper" function of the Law. That is to say Luther saw Law, in its proper use, as that which reveals to man his spiritual sickness--his sin, his lostness, his condemnation--and thus that which drives him to Jesus Christ as the only and final source of healing and saving grace. In like manner the "existential questions" in Tillich's Method are those questions which grow out of an analysis of the "brokenness" of human existence--those questions which ask for a healing answer to the dilemmas of finitude, of existential estrangement, and of the ambiguities of life. These questions are an expression of man's search for grace. On the other hand, Luther's presentation of the Gospel as the good news of God's forgiving love known and made real in and through Christ, is the methodological counterpart of Tillich's "Christian message" which presents the healing answers to the existential questions. Furthermore, it should be noted that both of our theologians see the Law (or the questions) as existentially and systematically prior to the Gospel (or answers). Just as a man is not interested in a physician unless he is aware of his illness (Luther), so no one is able to receive answers to questions which he has never asked (Tillich). For both men, the Law must be preached.[1]

We feel that we have demonstrated that Tillich's and Luther's understanding of the role of reason in the raising of the questions (the Law) and the presentation of the Christian answers (the Gospel) are systematically and substantially compatible.

181

Obviously Tillich has a more consistently positive attitude toward "reason," yet he agrees with Luther in that he sees the questions growing out of a "graced" situation just as Luther understood the "proper" use of the Law to be a work of the Holy Spirit. The next point is patently clear. Tillich is consistent with Luther in his insistence that the Christian answers (the Gospel) are always and only the product of revelatory grace, not of man's own self-creativity. Furthermore, it should be noted that while Luther insists that the distinction between Law and Gospel must be made, and while Tillich sees questions and answers as somehow independent, yet Luther refuses to drive a wedge between Law and Gospel and Tillich insists that questions and answers in correlation represent the "interdependence of two independent factors."[2] There is a polarity in the thought of both men at this point. One pole of their thought lives only in relationship with the other pole. If one pole is obscured or lost, the other is vitiated. This element of organic interrelatedness is seen in Luther when he asserts that both Law and Gospel are rooted in the Word of God, though they perform differing functions in the scheme of redemption. Luther expresses this element in another way when he states that the Gospel itself tends to bring a new kind of clarity to the Law and thus furthers its proper use. In Tillich's work this inter-relatedness is most clearly seen in what we have earlier referred to as the "feed-back" in his correlating method. "God answers man's questions, and under the impact of God's answers man asks them."[3] We submit that much criticism of Tillich grows out of a failure to understand this basic interrelatedness. When questions and answers are split from each other the questions become (incorrectly) autonomous.[4]

Within this polar methodological scheme, both men share one central focus--they are radically Christocentric. Both men insist that the solution to the human dilemma is God's work through revelation and grace, or the grace of revelation. And both

182

men hold that this revelation is to be understood in the light of the Christ event. For Luther the only true and saving knowledge of God comes through Christ. For Tillich "the New Being in Jesus as the Christ as our ultimate concern" is the material norm which controls the content of the systematic explication of the Christian message.

On the basis of our conclusions up to this point, we can also conclude that Tillich's Method does, in fact, safeguard Luther's central theological concern, that of "justification by faith alone." Since both questions and answers are the result of grace, salvation is wrought wholly by God.

> It should be regarded as the Protestant principle that, in relation to God, God alone can act and that no human claim, especially no religious claim, no intellectual or moral or devotional "work," can reunite us with him. It was my intention and it is my hope that this aim has been reached even if it has led to many quite "unorthodox" formulations in all parts of the system.[5]

On the basis of our study it seems clear, also, that a number of other significant parallels in substance could be traced, but these would lead us beyond the intent of this work. What we wished to show and think that we have shown is that, methodologically speaking, Tillich's claim to be a "Lutheran" theologian is, in fact, to be affirmed.

1. For an example from Tillich see his
Theology of Culture, pp. 207-208, where he recommends
that Christian educators and ministers use such voices
as Auden, Eliot, Sartre, and K. Menninger as a means
of undercutting the "complacency of those who assume
that they know all answers and are not aware of their
existential conflicts."

At this point we observe that Tillich, in
his total system, tends to subsume Luther's central
concern into a larger scheme of analysis. Luther's
primary search, religiously speaking, was that of
finding a gracious God--of finding a word of forgiveness which would redeem him from his guilt and condemnation. Tillich sees this "moral" anxiety as the focus
of concern in the closing of the Middle Ages, while
the end of the ancient world was characterized by
"ontic" anxiety (the anxiety of fate and death), and
the modern scene is marked primarily by "spiritual"
anxiety (emptiness and meaninglessness). (See his
Courage to Be, pp. 57-63.) Tillich, however, insists
that though one type of anxiety may be predominant,
the other types are also present and effective. Moral
anxiety is still a concern for Tillich. In fact, in
the light of his accent on "the courage to accept oneself as accepted in spite of being unacceptable"
(ibid., p. 164; cf. his sermon "You Are Accepted,"
The Shaking of . . . , pp. 153-163), it is most
surprising to find Robert Johnson writing: "the note
of forgiveness is . . . weakly sounded in Tillich's
system, . . ." (Op. cit., p. 123.)
    2. S.T., II, 13.
    3. S.T., I, 61. This interrelatedness is nicely
posed in Tillich's "Natural and Revealed Religion,"
Christendom, I (Autumn, 1935), 158-170: "The questioning for revelation must precede revelation, but this
questioning is not possible without a certain knowledge of the subject for which the question is asked.
That means: the questioning for revelation presupposes
revelation, and conversely: they are dependent on
each other. The beginning of the history of religion
is a question implying an answer and an answer imply-

ing a question" (p. 169).

4. Cf. Johnson, *op. cit.*, p. 115; McKelway, *op. cit.*, pp. 46, 70; G. F. Thomas in Kegley and Bretall, *op. cit.*, pp. 102-103; Marvin Fox, *op. cit.*, throughout his articles; and K. Hamilton, *op. cit.*, pp. 116 ff.

5. *S.T.*, III, 224.

BIBLIOGRAPHY

I. PRIMARY SOURCES

Luther, Martin. The Bondage of the Will. Translated
    by J. I. Packer and O. R. Johnston, Westwood,
    N. J.: Fleming H. Revell Co., 1957.
Luther, Martin. D. Martin Luthers Werke. Kritische
    Gesamtausgabe. Vols. 1 ff. Weimar, 1883 ff.
Luther, Martin. The Large Catechism. Translated by
    R. H. Fischer. Philadelphia: Fortress Press,
    1959.
Luther, Martin. Luther's Early Theological Works.
    Edited and translated by J. Atkinson. (Library
    of Christian Classics, Vol. XVI.) Philadelphia:
    The Westminster Press, 1962.
Luther, Martin. Luther: Lectures on Romans. Translated
    and edited by Wilhelm Pauck. (Library of Christian
    Classics, Vol. XV.) Philadelphia: The Westminster
    Press, 1961.
Luther, Martin. Luther's Works. (American Edition.)
    55 vols. planned. Edited by J. Pelikan and H.
    Lehmann. St. Louis: Concordia Publishing House,
    and Philadelphia: Muhlenberg Press, 1955--.
Luther, Martin. "Schmalkald Articles," Book of Concord,
    The. Translated and edited by T. G. Tappert,
    Philadelphia: Muhlenberg Press, 1959.
Tillich, Paul. Biblical Religion and The Search for
    Ultimate Reality. Chicago: The University of
    Chicago Press, 1956.
Tillich, Paul. A Complete History of Christian Thought.
    Edited by Carl E. Braaten. New York: Harper and
    Row, 1968.
Tillich, Paul. Christianity and the Encounter of the
    World Religions. (Columbia Paperback.) New York:
    Columbia University Press, 1964.
Tillich, Paul. The Courage To Be. (Yale Paperbound.)
    New Haven: Yale University Press, 1959.
Tillich, Paul. The Dynamics of Faith. (Harper Torch-
    books.) New York: Harper and Brothers, 1958.
Tillich, Paul. The Eternal Now. (Scribner Paperback.)
    New York: Charles Scribner's Sons, 1963.
Tillich, Paul. "Existential Analyses and Religious
    Symbols," Four Existentialist Theologians. Edited
    by Will Herberg. Garden City: Doubleday and Co.,
    Inc. 306-321.

Tillich, Paul. The Future of Religions. Edited by
    Jerald C. Brauer. New York: Harper and Row, 1966.
Tillich, Paul. "The Impact of Pastoral Psychology on
    Theological Thought," The Ministry and Mental
    Health. Edited by Hans Hofmann. New York:
    Association Press, 1960.
Tillich, Paul. The Interpretation of History. Trans-
    lated by N. Rosetski and E. Talmay. New York:
    Charles Scribner's Sons, 1936.
Tillich, Paul. Love, Power, and Justice. New York:
    Oxford University Press, 1954.
Tillich, Paul. Morality and Beyond. New York: Harper
    and Row, 1963.
Tillich, Paul. "Natural and Revealed Religion,"
    Christendom, I (Augumn, 1935), 158-170.
Tillich, Paul. The New Being. (Scribner Paperback.)
    New York: Charles Scribner's Sons, 1955.
Tillich, Paul. "The Problem of Theological Method,"
    Four Existentialist Theologians. Edited by Will
    Herberg. Garden City: Doubleday and Co., Inc.,
    1958, 263-282.
Tillich, Paul. The Protestant Era. (Phoenix Books.)
    Chicago: University of Chicago Press, 1957.
Tillich, Paul. "Relation of Metaphysics and Theology,"
    Review of Metaphysics, X (September, 1956),
    57-63.
Tillich, Paul. The Religious Situation. Translated
    by H. R. Niebuhr. (Living Age Books.) New York:
    Meridian Books, 1956.
Tillich, Paul. "The Religious Symbol," Symbolism in
    Religion and Literature. Edited by Rollo May.
    New York: George Braziller, Inc., 75-98.
Tillich, Paul. The Shaking of the Foundations. New
    York: Charles Scribner's Sons, 1948.
Tillich, Paul. Systematic Theology. 3 vols. Chicago:
    University of Chicago Press, 1951 ff.
Tillich, Paul. Theology of Culture. (Galaxy Books.)
    New York: Oxford University Press, 1964.
Tillich, Paul. "What is Wrong With 'Dialectic" Theology,"
    Journal of Religion, XV (April, 1935), 127-145.

II.   SECONDARY SOURCES

Adams, James L. Paul Tillich's Philosophy of Culture,
    Science, and Religion. New York: Harper and Row,
    1965.

Althaus, Paul. The Ethics of Martin Luther.
    Philadelphia: Fortress Press, 1972.
Althaus, Paul. The Theology of Martin Luther.
    Philadelphia: Fortress Press, 1966.
Armbruster, C. J. The Vision of Paul Tillich. New
    York: Sheed and Ward, 1967.
Baillie, John. Our Knowledge of God. (Scribner Paper-
    back.) New York: Charles Scribner's Sons, 1959.
Bainton, Roland. The Reformation of the Sixteenth
    Century. (Beacon Paperback.) Boston: The
    Beacon Press, 1952.
Boehmer, Heinrich. Martin Luther: Road to Reformation.
    Translated by John W. Doberstein and Theodore
    G. Tappert. (Living Age Books.) New York:
    Meridian Press, 1957.
Bouyer, Louis. The Spirit and Forms of Protestantism.
    Translated by A. V. Littledale. (Meridian Books.)
    New York: World Publishing Co., 1964.
Braaten, Carl. "Paul Tillich As A Lutheran Theologian?"
    An unpublished paper read at Lutheran School of
    Theology, Maywood, Illinois.
Brauer, Jerald C. "We Have This Ministry," Lutheran
    Social Welfare Quarterly, V (December, 1965),
    3-39.
Brown, D. M. Ultimate Concern: Tillich in Dialogue.
    New York: Harper and Row, 1965.
Brunner, Emil. The Divine Imperative. Translated by
    Olive Wyon. Philadelphia: The Westminster
    Press, 1947.
Carlson, Edgar M. The Reinterpretation of Luther.
    Philadelphia: Westminster Press, 1948.
Clayton, John P. The Concept of Correlation: Paul
    Tillich and the Possibility of a Mediating
    Theology. Berlin and New York: Walter de Gruyter,
    1980.
Cobb, John B. Living Options in Protestant Theology.
    Philadelphia: The Westminster Press, 1962.
Copleston, Frederick. A History of Philosophy. 7
    vols. (Image Books.) Garden City: Doubleday
    and Co., Inc., 1962--.
Cox, Harvey. The Secular City. (Macmillan Paperback.)
    New York: Macmillan Co., 1965.
Cranz, F. Edward. An Essay on the Development of
    Luther's Thought on Justice, Law, and Society.
    Cambridge: Harvard University Press, 1959.

189

Davies, Rupert E. The Problem of Authority in the
    Continental Reformers. London: The Epworth
    Press, 1946.
Dillenberger, John. God Hidden and Revealed.
    Philadelphia: Muhlenberg Press, 1953.
Dillenberger, John. Martin Luther. (Anchor Books.)
    Garden City: Doubleday and Co., Inc. 1961.
Dreisbach, D. F. "Paul Tillich's Hermeneutic,"
    Journal of the American Academy of Religion,
    XLIII (March, 1975), 84-94.
Elert, Werner. The Christian Ethos. Translated by
    Carl Schindler. Philadelphia: Muhlenberg
    Press, 1957.
Enquist, Roy. "The Living God: A Study of the
    Contemporary Discussion on Law and Gospel in
    Lutheranism." Unpublished Ph.D. dissertation,
    Union Theological Seminary, 1960.
Fenton, J. Y. "Being-Itself and Religious Symbolism,"
    Journal of Religion, XLV (April, 1965), 73-86.
Fischer, Robert H. "A Reasonable Luther," Reformation
    Studies. Edited by F. H. Littell. Richmond:
    John Knox Press, 1962.
Ford, L. S. "Appropriation of Dynamics and Form for
    Tillich's God," Harvard Theological Review,
    LXVIII (January, 1975), 35-51.
Forell, George W. Ethics of Decision. (Muhlenberg
    Paperback.) Philadelphia: Muhlenberg Press, 1955.
Forell, George W. Faith Active in Love. (Augsburg
    Paperback.) Minneapolis: Augsburg Publishing
    House, 1954.
Forell, George W. "Law and Gospel," A Reexamination
    of Lutheran and Reformed Traditions-III.
    Published jointly by Representatives of the
    North American Area of the World Alliance of
    Reformed Churches holding the Presbyterian
    Order, and the U.S.A. National Committee of
    the Lutheran World Federation, 1965, pp. 29-41.
Forell, George W. The Protestant Faith. Englewood
    Cliffs, N. J.: Prentice-Hall, Inc., 1960.
Forell, George W. "The State as Order of Creation,"
    God and Caesar. Edited by W. A. Quanbeck.
    Minneapolis: Augsburg Publishing House, 1959,
    pp. 29-52.
Fox, Marvin. "Tillich's Ontology and God," Anglican
    Theological Review, XLIII (July, 1961), pp.
    260-267.

Gerrish, B. A. Grace and Reason. Oxford: The
      Clarendon Press, 1962.
Gerrish, B. A. "To the Unknown God: Luther and
      Calvin on the Hiddenness of God," Journal of
      Religion, LIII (July, 1973), 263-292.
Grimm, Harold J. The Reformation Era. New York:
      The Macmillan Co., 1965.
Haile, H. G. Luther: An Experiment in Biography.
      Garden City: Doubleday and Co., Inc., 1980.
Hamilton, Kenneth. The System and the Gospel.
      New York: The Macmillan Co., 1963.
Heidegger, Martin. An Introduction to Metaphysics.
      Translated by Ralph Manheim. (Anchor Books.)
      Garden City: Doubleday and Co., Inc., 1961.
Holl, Karl. The Cultural Significance of the
      Reformation. Translated by K. and B. Hertz
      and J. Lichtblau, with an introduction by
      W. Pauck. (Living Age Books.) New York:
      Meridian Books, 1959.
Johnson, Robert C. Authority in Protestant Theology.
      Philadelphia: The Westminster Press, 1959.
Kähler, Martin. The So-Called Historical Jesus and
      the Historic Biblical Christ. Translated with
      an introduction by Carl E. Braaten. (Seminar
      Editions.) Philadelphia: Fortress Press, 1964.
Kaufmann, Walter. Critique of Religion and Philosophy.
      (Anchor Books.) Garden City: Doubleday and Co.,
      1961.
Kegley, C. W., and Bretall, R. W. (eds), The Theology
      of Paul Tillich. New York: The Macmillan Company,
      1956.
Kelsey, D. The Fabric of Paul Tillich's Theology.
      New Haven and London: Yale University Press, 1967.
Kostlin, Julius. The Theology of Luther. Translated
      from the second German edition by C. Hay. 2 vols.
      Philadelphia: Lutheran Publication Society, 1897.
Langford, Thomas. "A Critical Analysis of Paul Tillich's
      Method of Correlation." Unpublished Ph.D.
      dissertation from Duke University, 1958.
Lindberg, Carter. Luther's Concept of Love. Unpublished
      Ph.D. dissertation from the University of Iowa,
      1965.
Lohse, Bernhard. Ratio and Fides. Göttingen: Vandenhoeck
      and Ruprecht, 1958.
Lohse, Bernhard. "Reason and Revelation in Luther,"
      Scottish Journal of Theology, XIII (1960), 337-365.

191

Lunn, Arnold. The Revolt Against Reason. London:
    Eyre and Spottiswoode, 1950.
Lyons, James R. (ed.). The Intellectual Legacy of
    Paul Tillich. Detroit: Wayne State University
    Press, 1969.
Macleod, A. Tillich: An Essay on the Role of Ontology
    in his Philosophical Theology. London: Allen
    and Unwin, 1973.
McDonough, Thomas, O.P. The Law and the Gospel in
    Luther. London: Oxford University Press, 1963.
McGiffert, Arthur C. Protestant Thought Before Kant.
    (Harper Torchbooks.) New York: Harper and
    Brothers, 1961.
McKelway, Alexander. The Systematic Theology of Paul
    Tillich. Richmond: John Knox Press, 1964.
Martin, Bernard. The Existentialist Theology of Paul
    Tillich. New York: Bookman Associates, 1963.
Morgan, J. "Religion and Culture as Meaning Systems:
    A Dialogue Between Geertz and Tillich," Journal
    of Religion, LVII (October, 1977), 363-375.
Nelson, J. W. "Inquiry into the Methodological
    Structure of Paul Tillich's Systematic Theology,"
    Encounter, XXXV (Summer, 1974), 171-183.
Niebuhr, Reinhold. The Nature and Destiny of Man.
    One vol. edition. New York: Charles Scribner's
    Sons, 1955.
Niebuhr, Richard R. Schleiermacher on Christ and
    Religion. (Scribner Paperback.) New York:
    Charles Scribner's Sons, 1964.
Niesel, Wilhelm. The Gospel and the Churches.
    Translated by David Lewis. Philadelphia:
    Westminster Press, 1962.
Nygren, Anders. Agape and Eros. Translated by Philip
    Watson. One vol. edition. Philadelphia:
    Westminster Press, 1953.
Oberman, Heiko. The Harvest of Medieval Theology.
    Cambridge: Harvard University Press, 1963.
Palmer, Russell. "Karl Barth and the Orders of Creation:
    A Study in Theological Ethics." Unpublished Ph.D.
    dissertation from the University of Iowa, 1966.
Pauck, Wilhelm. The Heritage of the Reformation.
    Glencoe: The Free Press of Glencoe, Inc., 1961.
Pauck, Wilhelm and Marion. Paul Tillich: His Life and
    Thought, Vol. I, Life. New York: Harper and Row,
    1976.

Pelikan, Jeraslov. From Luther to Kierkegaard.
    (Concordia Paperback.) Saint Louis: Concordia
    Publishing House, 1963.
Pinomaa, Lennart. Faith Victorious. Philadelphia:
    Fortress Press, 1963.
Prenter, Regin. Spiritus Creator. Translated by John
    Jenson. (Muhlenberg Paperback.) Philadelphia:
    Muhlenberg Press, 1953.
Rome, Sydney and Beatrice. Philosophical Interrogations.
    New York: Holt, Rinehart and Winston, 1964.
Rowe, William L. Religious Symbols and God: A Philosophical
    Study of Tillich's Theology. Chicago: University
    of Chicago Press, 1968.
Rupp, Gordon. The Righteousness of God. London:
    Hodder and Stoughton, 1953.
Scharlemann, R. P. Reflection and Doubt in the Thought
    of Paul Tillich. New Haven and London: Yale
    University Press, 1969.
Scharlemann, R. P. "The Scope of Systematics: An Analysis
    of Tillich's Two Systems," Journal of Religion,
    XLVIII (April, 1968), 136-149.
Scharlemann, R. P. "Tillich's Method of Correlation:
    Two Proposed Revisions," Journal of Religion,
    XLVI, 1966.
Schrader, Robert. The Nature of Theological Argument:
    A Study of Paul Tillich. Missoula, Montana:
    Scholars Press, 1975.
Schultz, Robert C. Gesetz und Evangelium in der
    lutherischen Theologie des 19. Jahrhunderts.
    Berlin: Lutherisches Verlagshaus, 1958.
Schwiebert, E. G. Luther and His Times. Saint Louis:
    Concordia Publishing House, 1950.
Seeberg, Reinhold. Text-Book of the History of Doctrines.
    Translated by Charles Hay. One vol. edition.
    Grand Rapids: Baker Book House, 1961.
Thatcher, Adrian. The Ontology of Paul Tillich. New
    York: Oxford University Press, 1978.
Thomas, George F. Religious Philosophies of the West.
    New York: Charles Scribner's Sons, 1965.
Thomas, John H. Paul Tillich: An Appraisal. Phila-
    delphia: Westminster Press, 1963.
Watson, Philip. Let God Be God! Philadelphia:
    Muhlenberg Press, 1947.
Whale, J. S. The Protestant Tradition. Cambridge:
    University Press, 1955.

Wheat, Leonard F. _Paul Tillich's Dialectical Humanism_:
     Unmasking the God above God. Baltimore: John
     Hopkins University Press, 1970.
Williamson, C. M. "Tillich's Two Types of Philosophy
     of Religion: A Reconsideration," _Journal of_
     Religion, LII (July, 1972), 205-222.